Table of Contents

]

ts,

By Anthony Abiola Dada
(Aka Tony Biola)

The GPS System
7 Universal Principles for
Growing Personal Success

First published in 2014 by R-World Ents Ltd

Cover and Graphics design by Marlon Ruddock, Imagocracy Limited"

ISBN 978-1-63068-251-4

Acknowledgements

Just over 20 years ago having lost virtually everything I owned, I prayed that my life might have new meaning and purpose. I acknowledge first and foremost my God who answered that prayer and has blessed my life since then so abundantly.

To Miss D.A (Divinely Appointed) Serah Lister, you truly were Divinely Appointed to nudge me towards writing this book and it just wouldn't have happened without you, Thank you for being you.

I'd also like to thank Raymond Aaron, Lori and the entire team for an incredible 10x10x10 programme that I used to write this book, as well as Chris Coney, Viv Oliver and Marlon who came to the rescue in the nick of time.

Last and most important of all I would like to acknowledge you for deciding to pick up this book to discover how you can find and Grow your Personal Success.

Nuff Luv
Tony Biola

Foreword

The most difficult task in life is answering why am I here, what meaning can I give to my life's purpose, and how can I carve a successful life for myself. Believe it or not, most of us ponder this question at a very early age, many of us before we reach 10.

By asking this question early on in life, many of us have gone on to commit a critical error without ever realising that this error, if not redressed, will impact the rest of our life. What is this error?

Instead of exploring often latent gifts, talents and abilities, many of us allow others to dictate the direction our lives take. In essence, we exchange our personal roadmap for success, whilst still in the process of defining and exchange it for one given to us by mum, dad, grandparents, uncle or auntie, other family members, friends, or our primary or secondary school teacher(s). What's surprising is that this new roadmap is often based purely on nothing more than a mere opinion.

We then start living our life according to this new roadmap— which more often than not leads us to a dead end.

In this book, Anthony shares, through his own search for success, 7 universal principles for success which were first introduced to him by his mentor 30 years ago. These principles are illustrated through real stories from 7 of his mentees over a 20-year period, some of whom have come from disadvantaged backgrounds. Through his work and research he has discovered that young people just want to be successful, just like the rest of us, and it is simply this powerful desire that drives many down the wrong road, or even worse along the path to self-destruction.

He has worked as head of a centre of excellence College within Further Education as part of a 200 million pound project to establish 400 excellence training centres across the UK, as well as been fortunate enough to engage in meetings with employers such as the head of Apple UK, Loreal, Yamaha and a host of others. As a result, Anthony has concluded that the education system is forcibly going through a radical, rapid evolutionary change. This change, however, at the same time offers a wonderful opportunity to young people, an opportunity where for the first time they can explore their natural gifts, talents and abilities as well as learn skills that support their uniqueness, once discovered. The world today no longer wants workers doing a good job—the world is crying out for people who want to make a unique, meaningful contribution, people who want to make a positive difference.

This book introduces universal principles that support this global new education. Learn them, apply them and you become unstoppable as well as sought after globally for your value, as he illustrates through some of the stories of his mentees, which include his own children.

Raymond Aaron

NY Times Bestselling Author

Introduction

In the 20-plus years I've spent working with, nurturing and investing in young people and their talents, one thing I have learnt from them which I cherish most is the importance of "Keeping it Real". Why? Because I have learnt they almost have a sixth sense that is able to detect B.S. (cow dung). Once they get a whiff of that from you, you have lost them and it is one of the hardest jobs to win their trust back again. So whenever I engage with a young person and there is an opportunity to engage and relate over a period of time through a course or project, I always ask them very early in the relationship "Can we keep it real between us?" If the answer is "yes", which it usually is, we have just done our very first "deal" or "agreement", call it what you will, but make no mistake both parties know a deal has been made and are now watching the other to see if they'll keep or break the deal. This forms a solid foundation upon which our relationship can grow. At the end of the day, it is all about the "Relationship".

So my mantra is "Keep it real" first with yourself and then with others.

Having said that, may I state for the record that as part of this relationship between the two of us, as you read through the pages of this book, I will be "Keeping it real", so if you have a problem with that please read no further.

You've probably gathered by now that this book is aimed primarily, but not exclusively at young people who are starting out on their life journey seeking that path that leads to success. However, I believe that anyone who has taken the decision to want to grow and discover more of the latent possibilities which lie within each of us will find this book useful. So there is no age bracket; this book is intended for the person who is still young at heart, open to discovering the wonderment of living a fulfilled life with all that it has to offer. This book is for the person who is at the early stages of their journey on the road to self-discovery. This book is for the person who still has more questions than answers in relation to themselves and how they want to show up in the world. This book is for the person who intuitively feels deep within themselves that they are a star, that they are here to shine, to be somebody, to do something to make a contribution to this thing called life.

This book is not for the person who wants to spend—and I repeat SPEND—as opposed to invest the majority of their life in the pursuit of money, usually at the expense of meaningful rich relationships. I pause here to point out that though there is nothing wrong with having lots of money, the question is how much of YOU are you willing to trade, to give up, just to "get that bread". This book has been written for the person who is seeking success in a richer, deeper sense, seeking fulfilment, seeking to live an abundantly rich life. You see, the truth is that setting and pursuing financial goals alone is the most dangerous thing a person could ever do and will surely lead to ruin.

In this book, I will illustrate why and how to ensure that rather than tread the path to ruin you find your own unique path that leads to your success. The book has also been written for the person who seeks on a daily basis to do what brings them the greatest sense of joy, because they are 1) Doing what they love; 2) Doing what they are passionate about; and 3) Doing what they are good at. You could therefore be 15 or in your late 30's, 40's or 50's, having lived life in the rat race and come to that point of awakening when you realise that this can't be all that there is to life. In summary, this book has been written to reintroduce you to the real you that was born to be successful. It's time to "wake up everybody, no more sleeping in bed, no more backward thinking, time for looking ahead" (the lyrics in one of my favourite songs). This will be the first of a series of gifts from me to you. Register if you would like a copy of my forthcoming single "Wake-up", which I will be recording as part of my album in 2014. To register go to:

http://www.growpersonalsuccess.com

Now it's your time to be a star.

So why am I writing this book? The truth is I am really not qualified to tell you or anyone else how to find and grow personal success. However, from a very young age I was very curious about this thing called life and so over 30 years ago I began a journey which would lead me to many personal great discoveries. These personal insights, discoveries and theories led me to begin the conducting of "experiments" as a means of testing and proving these discoveries for myself. It is the most poignant of these discoveries which I have chosen to share with you in this book, with the sole purpose of illustrating 7 Universal Principles based on timeless ancient wisdom which can be implemented on a daily basis to personally grow success in your life.

These principles — if considered, studied and applied — will yield amazing fruits in your life very (and I mean very) quickly as I have written this book as a practical tool, distilling my 30 years of experience into a concentrated version for you. I have also illustrated each principle in a practical way through real events, revealing the impact they had on the young student or mentee concerned.

A wise man learns from other people's mistakes and successes — so my intention behind the use of these case studies is that they may cement your understanding of the principle.

The concept behind the GPS System (Grow Personal Success) is that it starts with you and starts exactly where you are. Accepting and recognising that you already have the success gene inside of you and you simply need to discover it through exploring your own natural talent, gifts and abilities, and then giving attention to the most dominant of these to cultivate your own unique sense of what success means to you based on your values is the first step. This process is simply that—a process, which must be cultivated over time. However, before I launch into what the GPS System is all about, I would like to share a short story that will put the contents of this book into context.

Chapter 1

The Story Begins with My First Confession

"The seed contains within it the oak tree"

This story is of a young boy nicknamed "Smiler" (as he always wore an infectious smile) living in London over forty years ago. He was born to African parents who had travelled to the UK in the 1960's. Smiler's father had come to study law with the intention of returning home to Nigeria to practice law. They were a close-knit family that kept to themselves due to the racism and prejudice that existed in those days – not just the obvious racism between whites and blacks, but within the black community itself mainly between Africans and West Indians. These were hard times and Smiler's parents definitely felt the pressure. Considered by Smiler as quite a hard man, his father had been brought up in a little village in Nigeria where he had experienced hardship working on a farm as a child. However, through strict discipline, focus and sacrifice he had found a way to leave Nigeria as a young man and made it to the UK, the only member of his family at the time to ever have achieved such a feat. In those days, that was an accomplishment that really took some doing.

Life for Smiler, however, was very different. He knew nothing of that African life as he was born in the UK and so like many other children born to British immigrants, he was living a life that his parents viewed as very privileged compared to where they had come from.

As a young child, he soon found he had a passion for music and loved listening to music on the radio and on the TV. He craved for it anywhere he could tune in, especially as at that time the family did not own a record player. One of his most loved artists was a relatively new young singer at the time called Michael. Michael sang as part of a group called "The

Jackson 5" and was really, really good. He would later become one of the world's greatest artists known as "Michael Jackson".

By the age of 7 or 8, Smiler realised he also loved to sing and use to go around the house often singing in his usual carefree adolescent way, as young kids often do.

By the time he was 10, he found that this interest in music had developed to an interest in song writing as well and soon he found himself inspired with floods of melodies for new songs. These ideas would often come to him at the weirdest of times right when he was in the middle of doing something else. What he often discovered was that if he didn't capture the melody by way of a recording, it would often be lost forever, as the idea, melody and inspired lyrics he found would desert him as quickly as they came.

So often he found himself making a mad dash to the living room to press record on the "Ghetto blaster" (That really was what they were called back then) which was the name used to describe the portable tape recorder which his uncle had recently bought for the family because of his love for music. There were no mobile phones to record on in those days.

Smiler loved music with a passion; the more he sung, the more new melodies and lyrics would just flow into his mind, and the more he would find himself dashing downstairs from his bedroom to the living room to press "record" so as to capture these melodies and chorus lines.

However, unbeknown to Smiler, there was a real big problem looming. You see, his parents were from Africa. More importantly, being of Nigerian parentage, to them preparing for a good successful life revolved around "facing your books", which was a term often used by his father, which loosely translated basically meant focus on your studies to the exclusion of everything else — and he meant just that, everything. No playing, no friends, no kicking back watching TV for hours, and certainly none of this music stuff. It was a strict regime.

His dad approached life with westernised aspirations; he had left the luxury of a warm climate, where he had a relatively good job, lots of friends and family members around him. He had educated himself to a high standard and so as a result was a sought after teacher who got paid well. As a result, he had good disposable income and so was able to enjoy his life being seen as successful amongst his peers and within his community.

However, he had sacrificed all this to pursue becoming a lawyer. He had saved hard to amass the money needed to purchase a plane ticket to London. On arrival, he went through further hardships and challenges and soon realised that the impression he had formed of the UK was not how it really was, but he was determined because he wanted to be a lawyer. He went through still further hardship as he tried to settle in this strange new environment. Getting accommodation was hard in those days. Landlords would openly display signs saying "No blacks, No Irish and No Dogs". Getting a job was hard, and he ending up having to take a job for which he was overqualified. In his eyes he had paid a big price to be in the UK and continued to pay that price on a daily basis. So from his perspective, his children ought to be eternally grateful for the new life he had created for them through his sacrifice, and the price he was paying.

So here Smiler was, totally oblivious to the challenges of being born and living in Africa, without a care in the world, living a happy go lucky life, as most primary school kids born and raised in England do. One morning, which seemed like any other, Smiler got up and went to the bathroom to freshen up so that he could go and start his house chores before school. As he made his way to the bathroom, he was humming to himself as he was in good spirits this morning.

All of a sudden, he got a flash of inspiration as the humming turned into quite an attractive melody. Making a mad dash to the living room with this new melody in his head, Smiler was about to push the door open, as he was in a hurry and didn't want to forget this melody. Suddenly, he saw that the door was closed, so he clasped the door handle, turned the handle to open the door and to his surprise, the door was locked. He couldn't believe it. He then realised in an instant what had happened; this was his dad's doing.

During the night whilst he was in bed, his father had put a lock on the living room door to stop him and his sister from watching TV and listening to music. His dad didn't like the fact that he liked music and this act would contribute towards their ever-estranged relationship. "How could someone be so cruel" he thought to himself. In that moment, Smiler realised how important music was to his life. He was determined that he would find a way to continue his music — he would raise some money so he could buy his own tape recorder, he would find a way, anyway to get that happiness and joy he obtained through his music and singing.

Unbeknown to both Smiler and his father, Smiler would later look back at this incident and realise that this was one of the most important moments of his young life. Why? Because it was the moment he found his first passion.

Unfortunately for Smiler, things did not improve. By the time he was approaching his teens the relationship between father and son was deteriorating fast. With the harsh restrictions imposed at home, Smiler used his time at school as playtime, mainly with his friend Christopher, but his was a playtime that lasted all day long, 5 days a week. Naturally this resulted in poor school grades. Life was starting to feel like cow dung, with increased tension at home and in school as now Smiler's academic achievements were in direct oppositions with his father's demands.

There was another problem. As he was getting older the tensions between Africans and Jamaicans living in the UK were increasing within many local communities where these 2 groups co-existed in large numbers.

Naturally this was also reflected in Smiler's school and on the council estate where he lived. He often found himself out numbered in on-going feuds where other youngsters of West Indian origin would "move" to him (meaning set to attack) for no reason other than the fact that he was of African heritage. On one occasion, a group of about 5 guys got into a fight with his father, which ended up with his mother getting involved and as a result also being assaulted. Smiler witnessed this and this was another defining moment in his early life. In that moment, he made a decision, a clear and conscious one. He decided that someone was going pay for this assault on his family, however long it would take, and in that moment he "marked" the guy who had attacked his mother—"That guy was gonna pay!"

These on-going feuds on the council estate, coupled with his dad eventually forbidding him to sing around the house, eventually created two dominant thoughts in Smiler's mind. The first—he had to figure a way to get out of this "hell hole of a house"; the second was he was going to teach that guy who attacked his mother a lesson he would never forget. He set about making a plan and one day with only a couple of hundred pounds to his name, he left home seeking refuge in a bed and breakfast hotel.

By now in his teens, he had made a few friends who were from a crew outside the area of Battersea where he lived with his family. They were different, a mixture of West Indians and Africans from South East London. The main difference here was the dominant culture was Nigerian and some of these guys were the type you really did not want to mess with. This crew had a reputation across London.

Smiler's situation regarding his feud with the local gang came to the attention of one of the leaders as things were getting worse; he was now having to "equip" himself every time he travelled to visit his mum and siblings back at home. The gang leaders summoned Smiler and interviewed him as to how this situation had come about.

A few days later, Smiler heard that a plan had been made and one Saturday afternoon 4 car loads of guys drove onto the estate armed with knives, metal bars, machetes and all sorts of weapons and set upon the local resident gang. The time for revenge had come and people were gonna pay for the hell they had put Smiler through.

That Saturday afternoon, the scenes that took place on that council estate in Battersea were not pretty, as you can imagine. Through the running battles, Smiler spotted the guy who had assaulted his mother and gave chase, followed by 2 others from his crew. The guy was running for his life and hate filled Smiler's mind as he gave chase; he was not going to let him get away. As the chase continued, the guy took a right turn and ran straight into 2 other members from Smiler's crew. They had him trapped. He was now surrounded. They slowly closed in on him. The enemy, who was called "P", was now squealing like a baby, had terror all up in his eyes and knew he was done for. Just as one of Smiler's crew was about to thrust a knife into his chest, in a split second something happened. Smiler suddenly pushed the knife away. Smiler hated this guy, yes he did, with a passion, but he didn't want him dead; the crew almost turned against Smiler in disgust barking, "What'd you bring us down here for then?"

Smiler pushed P against the wall, partly to save him from what was potentially a fatal encounter. Seeing this, the crew members then turned, walking off in fury with one of them saying, "Come man let's leave him to it; he wants his revenge". Smiler then set about P with his fists and gave him a battering. It was another one of those defining moments. His crew members were still mad. "Why you bring us all the way down here bruv and not let us take care of him", one shouted back as they walked off, but Smiler hadn't planned this far ahead. Yes he wanted revenge, but he didn't want anyone to lose their life. That was not how he intended it.

I share that story with you because that story of Smiler growing up in South London was the story of my adolescence — Smiler was me!

The Journey Begins

Soon after those events, I found myself homeless and trying to make sense of my life, questioning how I had gotten here and where I was going with my life. I had a random conversation with my mother one Sunday afternoon when I popped in to see her, knowing that my dad was out working. Little did I realise that this conversation was about to change my life's path forever.

It was a sunny Sunday afternoon. Things were cool now, and there no longer was any "beef" between the local gang and me. As I rang the buzzer and pulled the metal door, I thought how things were so very different now. I now had to be 100% responsible for myself, and it felt a little scary, actually very scary. But to my mind, I had no choice. It was either stay in my father's house where in my opinion things would only get worse and not better, or alternatively take my chances out there. As I knocked on the door I found it was already ajar so I walked in and made my way to the kitchen where mum was cooking Sunday dinner. I gave her a kiss as I sat down, chatting away about what I'd been up to that week.

I knew she was very worried about me; you see, I was the oldest and I knew it was hard for her seeing her first child that she had raised for 18 years now out there in that big bad world on his own. We spoke for a while and then somehow I started chatting about the fact that I was really not happy that I did not have a church to regularly attend, as now I was of no fixed address. My spiritual life had always been very important to me. Mum often used to chuckle as she reminded me of the time when I was 6 years old and during another one of those random conversations with her I started asking some deep questions (apparently for one so young) about God and the meaning of life. When the questions began to become too complicated to answer, mum had simply replied, "Son you can't question God, something bad will happen to you!" (an old African get out clause when adults have no answers available). The reply brought a shock response when she narrates how the story continued. I suddenly burst out in to tears. Mum quickly put down the saucepan she was washing in the kitchen sink and rushed over to me to stop the flow of tears and find out what was wrong. Through the tears I had reportedly blurted out, "How can I get to know God if I am not allowed to ask questions?" It was a profound statement and display of a questioning, probing natural disposition, one that unbeknown to me at the time would be a recurring theme throughout my life.

As our conversation continued, mum mentioned that one of her friends knew a gentleman who had just flown in from Ghana and was holding weekly meetings talking about life, and how to improve the quality of one's life. He was also holding 1-to-1 consultancy sessions to help people with their personal issues and problems. She asked me if I would be interested in coming along with her when he had the next gathering. I said "yeah sure" as I knew I needed some kind of help and direction because I had no clue as to where my current life journey was heading.

A couple of weeks later and there I was sat in this small room which had about 30 chairs all huddled together. Mum and I excused and squeezed our way past those already seated—we were late—as we made our way towards the nearest vacant two seats. We sat down, quickly made ourselves comfortable by peeling off our coats and as I settled in my seat I then began to listen to this tall looking slender gentleman speak. You could say he was like a motivational speaker/life coach; the only thing was hardly anyone knew those terms back in those days. He introduced himself as Bro Ishmael.

As he spoke he had a calm soothing disposition about him, yet spoke with authority. He was a charming guy and so within a few minutes he was cracking jokes and making us all laugh. You could tell he was very intelligent; I quickly found him to be a very interesting guy. As he spoke he used simple words, but his sentences were very thought provoking; he seemed to make so much sense as he spoke. As he spoke to us about living life and the skill involved in doing so successfully, one of the first things he said which pricked my ears was that he was a student of life and that nature was his teacher. I remember this because I recall not understanding what he meant by this statement. Many years later, I would come to understand fully. He spoke with a heavy African accent, so I had to pay attention so as to grasp every word he was saying.

When he was done speaking, some ninety minutes later, he sat down and then asked, "Are there any questions?" I was like "wow yes please!" You see, for most of the years that I had been attending my local Catholic church, one thing that had always bothered me was the fact that you couldn't ask questions, so I was not about to miss this opportunity to get some clarity on a few things concerning my relationship with my creator. I needed some answers to help me figure out where my life was going and how I was going to sort my life out, because at that moment it was set on a collision course to nowhere.

Before I knew it, my arm was raised and as my butt left the seat I tried to make myself visible from the back of the room.

I must have asked at least half a dozen questions over the next hour; I almost forgot that other people were there too. Towards the end of the questions session, he spoke, directing his comment towards me. If you would like you can see me afterwards and I can answer any further questions you may have". That was it—I was hooked. We did speak briefly afterwards and I asked a few more questions and then he said, "Perhaps you should attend one of my 1-to-1 consultations", as he observed there seemed to be no end to my questions. I was intrigued; many of the answers I received seemed to lead me to other questions. It was as if someone had turned on a tap inside of me. I somehow seemed to recognise the element of truth in what he was saying from deep within my soul, yet somehow my head, my left-brain in particular (where logic resides), was having difficulty processing and absorbing all this new info.

The thing that dazzled me the most though was that a few of the things he had shared were like nothing I had ever heard before at school or college, but yet as I listened, I kept getting what I call the "Eureka moment experience", time after time after time.

I had to come back the following week because I was sure that I would have at least a dozen more questions ready for this guy.

That was the beginning of what was to become a relationship that was to extend beyond 30 years; Bro Ishmael was soon to become my personal mentor and almost like another father. Over time, he would totally transform the way I thought about myself, the way I viewed the world around me as well as my role within it.

For the next couple of years, I was challenged greatly, as Bro Ishmael's approach to life was very different to the approach I had been exposed to from my father. One father was externally focused on the physical, with a strong desire on creating an image, projecting an important persona, chasing a career that was identified and pursued primarily because of the status it would provide him within his community. The other father's focus was on "spiritual" things (which I use here as another word for invisible). He took a more introspective approach to his life, determining first what he wanted to be, do and have (in that particular order) concerning his life and most importantly knowing clearly the reasons why those things were to be embodied, acquired or pursued. I was to later come to learn that making career and financial goals without setting goals in all the other dominant areas of one's life was probably the most dangerous thing a person could ever do because it sets you up for an imbalanced life, which is not sustainable — you eventually tip over.

One father lived with "nature being his teacher"; the other fathers' life was consumed by reading books, piles and piles of them.

One lived paying attention to their spiritual, mental, physical, social and emotional state. The other was only interested in books on the subject of LAW and becoming a lawyer, to the exclusion of almost everything and everyone else.

As I observed, compared, contrasted and pondered both these very different approaches to life, the burning question within me arose — which lifestyle approach did I think would lead ultimately to a happy and fulfilled life? I needed to decide which path I would take as each path was so very different from the other and would take me on completely different life paths. Eventually I made my choice.

Bro Ishmael and I soon embarked on an amazing journey, which would aid my journey of self-discovery. It became a journey of personal growth of heart, mind, body and spirit. I came to discover that "you don't know what you don't know until someone shows you". As simple and obvious as that may seem, it quickly taught me the need for incorporating at least a degree of humility into my life as I came to learn that the worst thing that can happen to a person is that another person knows stuff that once shared with you could better your life, but they simply chose to leave you in your world of darkness because you do not appear to be teachable. Now how sad is that? One is simply left quite literally in the dark.

I also came to learn that the opposite is also true, that when the student is ready and I mean not just intellectually but also heart-based, the teacher appears and so I soon came to realise that somehow by some strange happening the universe had seen me fit to become a student of Bro Ishmael. I had just left school, but my greatest schooling was just about to begin. I was soon absorbed with what I call this "Nu school" of thought, one that was based on the idea and belief that the purpose of one's life was not simply to attend school, leave school, get a (good) job, then stay at that job for 40 years, retire, draw a pension for a few years then lay down and die. No, not at all. This Nu school taught that life itself was a school, college and University from which all of our life experiences were simply opportunities provided through life itself to aid our growth in true knowledge and understanding about our own lives and the world around us. This Nu school also taught that as we as individuals come to grasp and understand this different concept of learning and growing, then we continue the learning upon graduating from Nu school in to the University of life. Life was a continual process of learning, growing and then learning anew as we discover even more about ourselves and the world around us and then grow again, all part of the great continuum.

I also came to learn that once the student is shown a new truth, and then gains knowledge and understanding of it, this often results in the student experiencing a paradigm shift. From that moment on, it is impossible for the student to act like they don't know, or live according to the old paradigm. "You gotta keep it real!" Remember? It makes no sense to lie to one's self, because if you do you eventually realise the only person who ultimately loses out repeatedly is you.

Over the years of study, I would come to learn that there is a universal desire shared by us all, from the small child to the adult. Every single person on this planet wants to become successful — that's it! And I have come to realise that it is fundamentally this lesson, "How to make a success of our life", that each of us is here to discover and learn — to learn how to BE-come Successful. It's really that simple, but here's the big problem. Depending upon our place of reference, we all have differing interpretations of what "SUCCESS" means to each of us. What the definition of success means to a young black teenager living on a council estate in South London is very different to the definition of success for an English girl whose father is a wealthy landowner and multi-millionaire.

The same is true for every other type of young person from any other social or economic background. The problem of lack of clarity of what success means creates an illusion, or a misconception of what success really is. This misconception must first be treated by creating a common working definition of what success is; one we can all feel comfortable with. In this book, I attempt to address this anomaly by creating a simple practical definition for success, which any young person can visualize and then use to Grow their own Personal Success, refining and adjusting as they go.

You see, the problem for many of us is that most of the people who know what the rest of us need to know in order to improve the quality of our lives are either too busy having a great time enjoying the fruits born out of what the know, or just too busy trying to take care of their own business because they have so much of it. They simply haven't got the time to show you or me how to improve our lives. In a few cases, I have witnessed that even during such a rare occasion where the sharing of a success message with a listening audience is given in relation to how to be successful and what needs to be done to take action, most people still appear to not get it and as a result discard both the teacher and the lesson. I have discovered that it is only those few who are willing to pay a price, make a sacrifice, toil seemingly in vain, at least initially and suffer a little pain, that ultimately discover the seed that grows into personal success.

Bro Ishmael once told me he was a global citizen from Africa and a true African cares and shares. So as a true African who cares and shares, he adopted me and became my mentor, introducing me to a whole new world of possibilities as I was willing to pay the price for self-discovery.

He introduced me to Timeless Universal Principles and natural laws, which govern all things in life, some of which I share in this book, like **Principle 1: The Law of Cause and Effect & Principle 2: As a Man Thinketh so is he.** He invited me to seek these ancient Truths for myself. "Let mother nature be your teacher", he would often say. "Like a mother loves her child so too does mother nature want only the very best for you", as is illustrated in **Principle 3: The Power of Love &Turning Passion –In2– Profits**.

I was to later realise being a student in this way would create a humility and respect for mother nature which in turn would help me to understand that to do something successfully or better still to become successful meant working collaboratively in cooperation with these universal principles and natural laws. I came to realise that you do not, in fact cannot, do it by yourself; you do things in partnership, hence the "co" before the words collaborate and cooperate, meaning joint effort. This is illustrated through **Principle 4: The Law of Gratitude and 5: The Law of persistence.**

Non-cooperation, whether conscious or not, or stubbornly going against these fundamental universal and natural laws could never and will never bring about sustained success. I mean seriously, can pigs fly? Of course not, however when you know where the airport is located and cooperate with the airport authorities, including the pilots who understand the laws of aviation, you can get your pigs on board a plane and your pigs can be flown through the sky to your desired destination.

So it is, with mother nature as your teacher, when you also cooperate she will reveal to you how your life can be abundantly rich, happy and fulfilled as illustrated through **Principle 6: The Law of High Quality Service.**

But, you must respect and honour her always! **Principle 7: Honour Thyself** shows you how.

Through the pages of this book, you will read the stories of some of my young students and mentees. Through these stories I share these 7 basic universal principles that I have learnt over many years of seeking how to improve the quality of my life so as to live a more fulfilled, happy and purposeful life. It is my firm belief that these universal principles and natural laws, once understood, respected and applied, will put you on the path that leads to the road which leads to the motorway that drives you to defining what success means uniquely to and for you. Through identifying, planting and growing the unique success seed that lies within you, whilst at the same time using it as your Personal GPS System, which plots your position in the world as well as your travel as you navigate your own magical journey, cultivating and growing your own personal success whilst making a unique contribution to the world.

Strange as it may seem, in working in this way rather than going after what I thought I wanted, I began to notice and experience that I instead began to attract things and experiences as well as people into my life.

Soon I was to find myself in the company of many people, some of whom I would play a part in shaping, nurturing, developing and investing in them as they discovered and grew their personal success, such as Leona Lewis, Alexandra Burke, JLS and Tinie Tempah, who became some of the UK's finest national and international music artists.

Others have made an impact in and outside of the UK, like Acie Lumumba who was originally introduced to me as a young man wanting to do music who enrolled in one of our Music courses at Urban Voice UK, the not-for-profit organisation I set up in 1993. I soon saw his real talent when he approached me asking me if I would be his mentor. Together we mapped out his blueprint that he has followed almost to the letter. He went on to become the Head of the Youth Parliament here in the UK and was invited onto a scholarship program at Harvard University in the United States, before returning to his native country of Zimbabwe where he is now an Honourable Member of the Parliament there. Likewise, there are many other stories. However, testing these principles on my two children (they have since forgiven me for this) has produced the most amazing results and has had the greatest impact on me by far. They are the main motivating factor behind the writing of this book as I have watched them grow, raising them as a single father.

Motivated by my mentor to not merely raise kids but to grow empowered children, one of my first experiments was to see if I could teach my son how to play chess. To my amazement, within 6 months he was playing chess quite well. However, the most shocking part of this experiment was that Joshua was actually playing chess quite well at the age of three. After basic lessons in financial literacy, he created and sold his first product at age 6, ran the London mini marathon at age 9, was in business selling products at age 11 turning over £500 per month with a sales team consisting of other school kids, and trained as a 400 meter runner for 7 years, often competing for his borough. He did this all whilst studying for his final school exams and training at the track 6 days a week, twice a day. As if all this was not enough, he then decided to follow in his father's footsteps by becoming a promoter and staged his first major event which was Wandsworth borough's first ever school prom. Of course it was a great success.

At the age of eight, his sister Jaie was not a very good singer, but loved singing and more importantly wanted to become a singer. Working with me as we travelled across the UK annually conducting 1000's of singing auditions for our Urban Voice National Talent competitions, she soon demonstrated that she was committed to her vision and soon became a good singer and then eventually a very good singer as well as a songwriter and artist development specialist, assisting me in putting together the course program that was used by pop group JLS, taking them on to stardom in the UK. She was offered a major recording deal, which saw her relocate to Nigeria, our native home and the home of the label. In less than 2 years after arriving in Nigeria, she had performed in concert with the likes of Chris Brown, international recording artist Mary J Blige, as well as performed for the Nigerian President (*http://bit.ly/1fzExpF*) All this whilst setting up an online women's lingerie business called Dime-Pink (http://www.dimepink.com)

which she developed in London and transferred to Nigeria where it was established. This was the beauty of having an online business and why she set it up together with her brother. You literally can take your online business with you to any country. This was done after supposedly taking time out, during which she wrote a fictional novel (*Soul Ties* by Jaie Dada, available on Amazon- http://amzn.to/1b104ms). After producing the manuscript, she then sourced and commissioned her book cover, found a publisher and got her book published whilst she was still only 20.

The interesting thing for me is that during subsequent conversations both children have told me that they put their achievements down to the cultivation of a success-oriented mindset, which was the backdrop to everything that was done within our home.

You too have talents, skills and abilities, which if you put to good use could find you being called to various parts of the globe to share your gifts and talents.

You have the computer software to design a program in your mind, the likes of which people and the world have never seen before. What are you waiting for? Learn the software called Success and write the program—your "successful life program" and let it be your operating system upon which you live your life. You then simply grow this personal success by embodying and living out your "successful life program".

As you now prepare to embark upon a journey with me looking at each of the 7 principles, I will support each principle through the illustration of real life stories of some of my young mentees and some of my own.

If you wish to study the principles further to cement them more deeply so that they become part of your lifestyle, please visit the website: http://www.growpersonalsuccess.comand

register for test paper of short questions after finishing each chapter. Through the website, you will also access further Grow Personal Success courses and material for those who want to achieve a personal transformational experience within a set period of time. These take the form of an 8 week and 12 week course, both of which carry a money back guarantee. A 1-day introductory workshop introduces you to these transformational courses.

For a complete and total transformation across all the 5 main areas of your life (physiological, psychological, spiritual, social & emotional, and financial/service) I have also put together a reading list of 12 books which I recommend you read (minimum 1 per month) once you have completed reading this book. You will discover that the books will support much of what has been introduced to you here whilst giving you the ability to reinforce and build on your learning at the "Nu School".

With all that said, let us now begin our journey together.

Chapter 2

Universal Principles

Universal Principles

Before we really get started, I think that it is important to define a few terms so that we can understand clearly what is meant when these words appear throughout this book. This book has the subtitle "7 Universal Principles for Growing Personal Success". Let us break these words down, starting with the word Universal. By this we simply mean that which is worldwide, present and operating everywhere involving everyone, like air. Next let us look at the word "principle". Here is the dictionary definition of the word principle: "A fundamental, primary or general law or truth from which others are derived".

The interesting thing about a principle is that it governs, overrides, or controls how something happens or works. Whether one is aware or not of the principle's existence or presence or its subsequent effects is totally irrelevant; your wishes or desires have no effect upon a principle.

So the book's subtitle "7 Universal Principles" therefore conveys that this book introduces 7 truths that if incorporated and applied to your life thus becoming a lifestyle, which will eventually impact your life, regardless of wherever you may reside in the world. Whether you do this consciously or not makes no difference.

However, being conscious of these principles, whilst adopting and embracing them into the fabric of your life, i.e. cooperating with them, will further enhance and increase the quality of your life experience.

A Paradigm

A paradigm can be described as a theory, hypothesis or a concept. An example of this is now given. Prior to 6th May 1954, the theory held by most people was that it was impossible for a human being to run a mile in under 4 minutes. When Roger Bannister achieved this, there was a shift to a new paradigm; a new reality had been created, born to replace the old. Why? Because what was once considered impossible was now possible and a paradigm shift was necessary as people now adjusted their belief to this new reality.

Natural Talents

We are all born with natural talents. These are things that we are just good at, not because we learnt or acquired a skill. I firmly believe that it is the role and duty of every parent to expose their child to as many different experiences early on in life with the sole aim of watching attentively to see what the child is naturally good at. For example, with my own son I began to notice at the age of two that he seemed to have excessive amounts of energy which people often commented on. As a result, I consciously decided to expose him to as many forms of sporting activities as possible. This energy eventually expressed as a natural talent for running (particularly long distances) as well as other sports that required stamina.

Abilities

Following from this realisation that he had this natural talent of excessive energy that expressed itself through his ability to perform well in sports, I then explored further by looking at what sports he found easiest and enjoyed the most. Together we discovered he had many abilities within a range of sport disciplines, from athletics, to football, to gymnastics. But through a process of further exploration, we determined together that running was the ability he would focus on, as it was the thing he enjoyed the most. Abilities then simply mean the things one can do easily.

Gifts

Gifts are the bringing together of both Natural Talents and abilities combined with the person's specific intention and willingness to simply give it away. To give away with the sole purpose that others might derive pleasure from that which is given. A classic illustrator of this was Michael Jackson. There are many great singers around the world and there are many great performers, but few could stir emotions like Michael Jackson when he sang and performed. I believe it was not just because he had a natural talent and ability, but even more important was the fact that when he performed he performed with the audience in mind, holding that childlike quality (which he never lost) of aiming to please throughout his entire performance and as a result transferred a gift to us whenever he sang or performed. Michael did this every single time and it was his human connection through his giving to his audiences his very best, this free gift shared during every performance, not just performing or entertaining, that made him so very special.

Looking for another example in more recent times, Usain Bolt has natural talent and ability; however, he is loved not just for his amazing ability to run so quickly but also for the performances he gives us before and after his races, such as the hand gestures and poses, amongst others. He doesn't have to do any of those things but he does. Those are his gifts to us, given for FREE because he wants to and we love him all the more for it. How many of us give our gifts when we are doing "our thing"? We'll talk about this in more detail later on in the book.

Success

The last term to define is the term success.

Now let's look at what we mean by the term Success. Two dictionary definitions are shown below:

1. The achieving of the results wanted or hoped for.
2. Something that achieves positive results.

Personally, I prefer the latter because the first definition could describe the achievement of a drug dealer who sells crack to his customer, which does not have the same fit when applied to definition two. There is a positive result in the short term, to obtaining money, but there are many knock on negative results that will also spring from this seemingly positive result depending upon the methods employed to obtain this money.

To further illustrate this, if drug dealing was full of benefits for all parties concerned, why are these transactions not carried out in full public view? Having spoken to many drug dealers, I am left curious as to why the desire of so many is more often than not to make enough money so that they can get out of the game? Could it be because the intent of the drug dealer does not promote positivity and deep down they know it?

My mentor shared his definition with me, which I personally prefer and would like to share with you:
Success is that which:

1. You enjoy doing
2. Honours you
3. Promotes life & positivity.

So let's go back to our example of Usain Bolt and see how well this definition fits:

1. Is he doing what he enjoys doing? Most certainly.

   Having lived with a young athlete and watched him subject himself to sometimes very painful training programs for seven years, when I often asked him "Tell me again son why do you put yourself through this", his reply would always be the same—"Because I love the buzz from everyone cheering as I run around the track and I love winning."

   When Usain Bolt ran and won the 100 meters at the 2012 Olympic games in London, 100's of millions of people around the globe stopped what they were doing to focus on this one man and the event.

2. Is he doing what honours him? The eruption from the stadium which reverberated around the world definitely illustrated this, coupled with the bestowing upon him of the Olympic gold medals which he obtained, countless sponsorship deals, interview request and TV interviews all illustrate without a doubt that the man is honoured throughout the world for what he does.

3. Does what he is known for promote life and positivity? By this I mean does it inspire, motivate, bring pleasure, and uplift his many tens of millions of fans? Again the answer is a resounding yes.

Now compare Usain Bolt to disgraced cyclist Lance Armstrong, who for many years seemed to display the 3 elements of our definition of success until a point came during his career when his actions and activities were found to bring dishonour to his name, and then like a deck of cards it all came crashing down.

Usain on the other hand literally oozes joy and happiness, always offering that cheeky friendly smile. You see, when you are doing what you love and it honours you, you feel good, proud, happy, accomplished and a host of other positive thoughts and feelings, which flow through your entire body. Giving new meaning to that old Jamaican saying "He who feels it knows it".

Now this illustrates a very interesting relationship between these 3 elements of success as per our new definition, that is that they are inexplicably linked—all 3 must be present in order to create the success that endures. Before pursuing any path towards any desired successful outcome, apply these 3 basic rules to your planned endeavour and they will also hold you in good stead.

I want to emphasise these 3 elements because truly they hold the key to success.

Doing what you enjoy doing

Most people do not take the time to pay close attention to identify the natural gifts, talents and abilities that they themselves possess, which is the first big fundamental error. Let me illustrate. For a moment, imagine if you could wake up every morning knowing that for the entire day you were going to be engaged in doing what you naturally love doing — what would that sensation feel like? I can almost see the smile forming on your face. "How did I know that?" I can almost hear you say. Well it's because I have posed that same question to many scores of people and seen that exact same response.

Let's look a little closer; at that very moment you entertained that thought, there was a shift on a number of different levels, actually on the mental, emotional and physiological levels, your whole being was in harmony with the idea and you know how good it felt. So why haven't you spent quality time with YOU to explore this good feeling in terms of considering what you would really enjoy doing, before rushing out to get a good qualification so that you can get a good job, so that you can earn money to live the quality life that you believe you deserve. Could it be because the idea of pursuing what you enjoy doing regardless of where it takes you as long as it honours you, promotes and supports life and positivity is one that is alien to you as well as most other people? Could it be because the spirit of fear is what is driving most people in the mass labour market? And what is F.E.A.R. – False Evidence Appearing Real.

The family unit, in whatever form that might take, is the first or at least should be the primary socialising agent where we learn all our norms, values, belief systems and above all receive love through our parent(s) and other close family members. Most parent(s) when raising children hold deep in their heart the desire for the child to have a better life than they did, which is noble. However based on the old type of thinking, this goal of a better life was considered to have been achieved mainly by ensuring that one had acquired lots of money. This viewpoint as I will soon illustrate is no longer the case in the new age.

To ignite that spark of what it is that you enjoy doing is and should always be the first step and this is easier the younger a person is, so I have found. Why?

Often the evidence of this first love, this passion can be traced back to one's childhood. However as one grows, this passion, if not nurtured, gets buried. So with age there is a gradual but continual distancing from what you enjoy doing till one day, if the pursuit of acquiring more and more money has been your only or main guiding compass, come adulthood you wake up one day and find yourself in a desert place, quite literally.

If you enjoy doing something, chances are you will spend more time doing it, this in turn will make you more skilled at it, which in turn will make you stand out when compared to others, not because you are a genius but simply because you've had more practice—it will honour you and as the old saying goes "Practice makes perfect". More on this latter.

The 3 types of people

I have noticed over my years of research that there appear to be three category types of people when it comes to success. They are broadly those who:

1) Don't know that something just happened – because they are asleep.
2) Watch what's happening, - because they are sleep walking, awake but still dreaming.
3) Make things happen using their Natural talents, abilities and gifts – They are aware of themselves and their surroundings and how they can influence both.

It may seem brutally honest, but it's true; these 3 categories do sum up most people and becoming successful starts first with you being real with yourself in determining which group you belong or wish to belong to, as it is my opinion that only those who are aware have a chance of being successful. Are you the type of person that is disinterested in most things? A term I often hear from young people on London streets is *"a waste man"*. Picture this for a moment—a person who can only be described as waste, i.e. that which is discarded, unwanted or left over, in terms of their appearance, energy, interest, enthusiasm, mindset, their whole constitution sums up to nothing but a big "0". However in my studies I have found that even the so-called *"waste man"* has an interest or a desire they want to fulfil. The aim should be to discover what this interest is as early on in life as possible and then make it one's focus. Actually in this new world and economy, the younger you are the better placed you are to ensure that you are in category three where people make things happen with success in mind as previously defined, which in turn promotes life and positivity.

This notion of doing something that promotes life and positivity can be further illustrated through the words of Nick D'Alosio, the young entrepreneur and founder of Summly, the service acquired by Yahoo for millions of dollars, who in one of his speeches urged young business leaders of tomorrow to seek out gaps in the marketplace, finding out everything they could about that gap and then owning it. Why? Because young people, he said, are uniquely positioned to solve the problems of tomorrow, having grown up in the new "technological revolution age". He went on to explain that your age simply does not matter if you have a great idea. He illustrated this by saying "I got a phone call from one of the richest men in Asia at aged 15".

Another example of a young person making things happen around them is young entrepreneur Emily Brooke, who in an article stated, "The key is to find your problem". Emily's company Blaze specialises in developing products for the urban cyclist. She had never planned or wanted to be an entrepreneur, but a love of cycling unexpectedly led her down that path.

"I got the cycling bug and in my final year when I had to design a product from start to finish, I decided to look at the challenges facing urban cyclists," she said.

"The key is to find your problem, understand your problem and only build something valuable if you're solving a problem you know better than anyone else." Emily said. She spent time speaking to bus drivers, the council and experts in road safety, before discovering the biggest threat to cyclists was vehicles not seeing them and crossing their path. "I knew exactly what problem I wanted to solve".

"Find a problem that you really are obsessed with and understand it better than anyone else, that's the only way to find a valuable answer. And do what you love, you'll do it and you'll love doing it and you'll be happy", she said.

Like Brooke, D'Alosio spent time finding out everything he could about the technology that would support his idea. That began with Google, books and online tutorials. But by the time his beta version was out, he was speaking to the Stanford Research Institute. "I had the idea," he said, "but I would never be as good as someone who did it for 20 years."

Nobody Else really matters – What is your definition of success?

We all want to be successful — that's a fact — but do you really know what you want to have, what you want to be and what you want to do. These are 3 of the most fundamental questions in the initial process of the art of learning what personal success means for you. However, I am amazed at how few of my students have ever asked themselves these questions. The easiest way for us to determine the answers to these questions is starting from the place of identifying WHAT IS IMPORTANT TO YOU? I now want you to undergo a short exercise and experiment to see if you do in fact know the answers to these 3 questions. This exercise is comprised of 2 parts. Register at http://www.growpersonalsuccess.com/ to access and download this exercise worksheet complete with examples.

Part 1: The "Right Brain exercise"
I would like you to find a quiet space where you will not be disturbed for at least 30 mins. If you can do this on a day that you're just chilling-out and therefore nice and relaxed, that would be great and the morning of such a day whilst relaxing with no important things to attend to is even better. Quickly without giving it much thought, list in bullet point form 10-12 things or goals that you currently consider to be

very important to you and your future. The list can be as long as you want, but should not contain less than 10 points, the longer the list the better. I call this the right brain exercise because here we are focusing on mental activity that has been scientifically proven to be activity that is conducted through the right side of the brain. This activity opens our mind up to ideas, visions and all forms of creativity. Once exhausted, we will move on to part 2 which, yes you've guessed it, I call the "left brain exercise".

Part 2: The "Left Brain exercise"

Here we are engaging the left side of the brain that has been scientifically proven to be responsible for linear thinking, problem solving, generally working things out and logical thinking.

Armed with your list of goals and things that are important to you, I now want you to sort this list into a list with your highest priority at the top and continue arranging your list in order of what is the next priority for you. You will find this exercise far more difficult than the first. Next to each priority as you list them, I'd like you to write why it's important to you. OK are we done? Great!

Let's now park this list for a moment and continue the journey through the book, because if you are anything like my students who have been on the Growing Personal Success coaching program, you may find that you change the list and its order dramatically after having read this book.

This is the first exercise undertaken by all my students on the GPS coaching/Mentoring program and in almost every case students find it a far more challenging and self-illuminating process than they originally thought as it forces them, often for the very first time in their lives, to really ask these probing deep questions through a mentally holistic process, engaging both sides of the brain consciously. Is it the first time you've asked yourself such personally probing questions? I do hope so as this will illustrate you are already benefiting from your investment in this book.

Through reading these universal principles for success and as you consider how they relate to you "personally", this will help you redefine your list as you realize that some of the "Why's" you previously listed are not so important to you after all and so as you read through this book you may as a result find yourself revisiting your list, often adjusting the priority listing. You may even find that some items get moved and placed lower down your list whilst others get taken off the list all together, being replaced by new priorities that you now discover through reading this book and engaging in this process are of higher value or importance to you. If you find that this is your actual experience, then this will be your hard evidence of our new definition of "personal success" taking shape and emerging from within you as you read this book. Literally as you read this book, you will begin to define or redefine your life-purpose.

This is because, for the majority of us, we do not realise that for many years what we have often considered as being important to us was merely our mind's unconsciously adopting or adapting many external influences, ideas, and suggestions communicated to us through a host of mediums around us such as parents and other family members, friends, teachers, TV and the media.

Together through this book, we will take you on a journey of self-discovery where you discover YOU more deeply, finding, defining and establishing what goals are important to you in the 5 most dominant areas of your life. This will be achieved through simply creating a space in which you will be given an opportunity to take time to study and get to know YOU, maybe for the very first time.

Now that you have created an image and an idea through your list that looks like personal success, what are you going to do about it? Remember you now understand the 3 types of categories of people that exist. It's the people that make things happen that succeed, so the dominant questions you must ask yourself on a daily basis must now be what can and do I want to make happen?

Pursue happiness not money

Daniel Priestley, in his excellent book *The Entrepreneur Revolution,* stated through one survey conducted in the USA that $80,000 per year per person was a significant number for maximizing happiness. In the study, more money consistently equalled more happiness up to $80,000 per year, but after that threshold, more money had very little impact on happiness at all. Yet how many people spend so much of their lives pursuing the illusion believing lots of money will make them happy, never to attain it and never getting to that point of realizing that money alone does not bring happiness, a sense of success or fulfilment.

Equipped with this new found realisation and knowledge, we will now continue our journey pursuing happiness and Growing Personal Success through the study of the 7 Universal principles.

Chapter 3

Principle 1:
The Law of Cause and Effect

Every effect is the result of a previous cause whether you are consciousof this or not. Therefore focus not on "effects" but "causes"

My mentor often advises me to look to nature as your teacher, so I shall do just that in illustrating this first principle.

The farmer knows this first universal principle of cause and effects only too well. He knows he must first be clear of what crop he wishes to harvest; then and only then when he is clear and sure does the physical work begin. The farmer knows he must set a plan and then cause a number of things to happen to bring about this desired effect.

He takes his seed crop and goes to work planting this seed. Then having planted this seed, he understands that he must now toil the land giving the seed all that it needs in order that the seed may take root to flourish and grow. This is the hardest part of the process as the work is hard and for a long period there no physical evidence appears that the toil is of any use; however, this is the principle of cause and effect in action. It is a universal principle and therefore not subject to what your eyes or other senses for that matter inform you, for the senses sometimes may deceive you. When you know and understand that this principle is at work, you can continue the intense labour required in any work, knowing that the work will eventually pay off, not because you want it to but because that is the law born out of this principle.

So I encourage you to put the work in only once you have identified and are assured of your dreams, visions, goals, and aspirations. Put the work in daily, diligently nurturing, cultivating your vision and in the right season things will begin to blossom. When others begin to falter, you will continue with strength because you know and understand this principle.

Having and growing personal success is the effect, the result you desire. Therefore what must you "do" or "cause" in order to achieve this desired effect is the question to be asked.

I am reminded of an old Jamaican proverb and lyric which says "Spit in the sky and it will fall into your eye". Simply translated what this means is that if you do something vulgar, it will come back to you eventually. This proverb perfectly illustrates the principle of "cause and effect" in operation through the natural law of gravity. The principle of cause and effect suggests that for every cause there is an effect. Similarly, the reverse is also true—for every effect there must be a cause, whether you see the cause visibly or not and whether you are conscious or unconscious of the principle in operation.

Therefore, if you consciously or unconsciously spit in the sky, you have created a "cause", for which there will be an "effect", which in this case is the spit falling into your eye.
This illustration, although somewhat crude, and its understanding is incredibly empowering because as we learn, understand and work harmoniously with this and other universal principles, we find ourselves quite effortlessly moving from a victim state to one that is empowered. This means that we benefit; paradoxically we achieve more through doing less. This principle can also be observed whilst watching martial artists fighting. Martial Arts simply translated means highly skilled fighter and as highly skilled fighters, those who study the martial arts have learnt how to use their opponent's moves, body, and energy (causes) against them by merely redirecting the opponent's

moves and energy flow into an effect or outcome that they initiate. Simply put, they interrupt their opponent's action (cause) by disrupting it and introducing a new cause that they initiate, thus creating a new effect or outcome, which sometimes can be quite comical to observe.

When we are not aware of this principle at work or blatantly disregard the principle, then it works against us. But understand that this is a principle that operates all the time and your mind begins to seek out this principle at work in your daily life. Try looking for it in operation as you go about your daily activities. You may be surprised how often you see the principle at work.

Understanding this first principle is extremely important.

My mentor taught me this lesson rather harshly in one of our first sessions; I will never forget the experience. I had scheduled to meet with him as he held regular consultation sessions, which looking back I now realise were private sessions with my mentor. I had decided to meet with him because of all the problems I had experienced and to an extent was still experiencing — fights at school, gang fights on my council estate and hostility at home between my father and I.

My mentor listened intently as I spoke during the meeting, then after I had finished he said "Son!" I said "yes". He continued, "Everything that happens to you, you either caused it or you allowed it". I responded "WHAT!" I was furious. I wanted to say to him, "After I come all the way down here and share all this personal stuff with you in the hope that you might be able to help me see something that I might be missing and that's all you can say?" But I didn't because African culture dictates that a young one is not disrespectful to an adult unless given very good cause and that was not the case here. So I made up some lame excuse and promptly left, but boy was I furious.

As the days passed, my anger subsided and I began to think about what he had said, but it made absolutely no sense to me. Why would he say such a thing to me? I had found him to be a nice guy, at least that's what I thought until this point and so I couldn't understand why he would upset me in that way.

A week had passed and it was now starting to bug me, so I decided I was going to eat humble pie and go back and see him and ask him why he had said such a hurtful thing to me. Remember my natural ability to probe through asking questions.

I called his PA and booked myself in to meet with him. It was now 7 days after that call. As I knocked on the door and was shown into his small office, I felt a little nervous about the confrontation that was about to occur.

I told him that I had been thinking about what he had said and did not understand and wondered if he could explain further as I realised I might have been a little hasty in my departure when last we met. He must have read my mind as I silently chuckled to myself as I listened to how cleverly I had masked over the real thoughts I had been having. He smiled, chuckled back and then said in his gentle and soft tone, "son". I replied "yes". He continued, "It is in fact true that everything that happens to you, you either allowed it or caused it to happen and unfortunately most do not understand this principle, one of the universal laws of life." He paused and then said, "Let me show you." He continued. "You were angry with all of these people and negative situations you have been experiencing, yes?" he inquired. "Yes", I responded, not sure where he was going. He continued, "And you had thoughts and images of how you would like to get back at them for all the hurt and pain caused to you, right?" "Yes", I said with conviction. "Well in those moments when you were having and entertaining those thoughts, you were causing and creating images in your mind which you fuelled with intense desire and so you created the perfect recipe for attracting negative experiences, and just like a magnet you attracted negative experiences into your world". "I was?" I asked, raising my voice slightly. "Yes", he said, "just like the person who uses saliva to create spit and then spits it out, it is the natural law of gravity which administers the effect of the spit falling back into your eye. Similarly when you have a negative thought charged with high emotion, you are beginning a creative process in your mind and guess what?" he asked. "What?" I responded, as he continued knowing I had no answer to offer. "The governing principle of cause and effect works there too". He paused.

I could not speak as my eyes widened and I began to take in what he had just said. *The law of cause and effect operates in my mind*, I thought to myself. He saw my state of amazement at what I had just heard and so continued, "Right there in that state of anger, you were creating in your mind these highly, emotionally charged thoughts and just as the misuse of the natural law of gravity draws the spit to you its creator so too does the misuse of the law of the mind draw to each and everyone of us that which we hold intently in our minds. So you see son, it was you that was creating and thus drawing many of these negative experiences into your life just like the painter paints his picture".

The Roots Conquest Story

Back in 2003, Urban Voice UK was in its infancy, having just been set up as a not-for-profit organisation earlier that year. Unusually, within 3 months of being set up, the organisation received £75,000 in funding from the Arts Council to stage the Urban Voice National Talent competition, which had been running and growing in size since its humble beginnings way back in 1998 in South London.

It was now September and we had been working with our new winners Roots Conquest, who had won the competition the previous year. These three young guys had entered the competitions as individuals but then joined forces to blend their styles together. Their music was of a roots reggae style and their lyrics were all about peace and love. A "Conscious vibe" is how the boys described their music.

I had negotiated a deal with Island Records over at Universal, securing both a sponsorship deal for Urban Voice UK plus a recording deal for Roots Conquest as part of their prize as winners and everyone was very excited.

I met with the guys on several occasions as we got to know each other and bonded after their victory. After a few meetings, I shared my plan with them in terms of the deal I had secured at Island, which consisted of them recording an EP at the legendary Island Studios where Bob Marley had done his many recordings. This EP would then be presented to Nick Gatfield, whose was running the label at the time, for consideration in terms of signing the group to the label.

The recording project began and over the weeks that the sessions took place we could tell that we were developing quality tracks. It was an amazing experience, almost unbelievable. I had started on this journey to use music and creativity as a means to engage with young people more than ten years prior with no money and no resources of any sort, just the belief and the mantra from my mentor that "If you can visualize it then it's possible" and now here I was about to go in to Island records with my recording artists. Who would have thought that from following through on this idea and subsequently staging the competition ("the cause"), I, along with ROOTS CONQUEST would be having such an amazing experience, which was the "effect."

At the end of the recording project, we were ecstatic. We had 5 tracks produced and the tracks sounded "Heavy" (in our opinion). The tracks were now ready to present to Nick Gatfield, a man whom I had now grown a great deal of respect for as not only had he sponsored the recordings, but he also sponsored the competition with real cash. The first and only label to ever support Urban Voice UK in this way. Register at http://www.growpersonalsuccess.com to receive a FREE track from the EP as a bonus gift.

The meeting was set up and I was so excited I hardly got any sleep the night before. Prior to this meeting, the boys from Roots Conquest had agreed in principle on management terms and I had informed them that I would draw up contracts for them to sign after the meeting with Nick. It was all moving so very quickly.

As I stepped up to the receptionist at the offices of Island Records, I was asked to wait and told that Mr Gatfield would be informed of my arrival. It felt like a 30 minute wait, but as I rose out of my seat to follow his PA, I glanced at the clock and realised that I had only been sitting there for a few minutes. Mr Gatfield greeted me at the door with a friendly smile. He seemed genuinely interested in what I was doing within the community and my aspirations to put together an album project of aspiring UK urban artists—The Urban Voice, i.e., an album showcasing the voices of youth from across the UK that would be distributed through a label such as Island. He explained his commercial position and support for what I was doing, but went on to say he did not feel that the tracks were a sure bet and so for that reason and that reason alone he would not be willing to sign the guys to his label.

> *It's not what happens to you but how you respond*
> *to what happens to you!* Bro Ishmael Tete

I left Mr Gatfield's office very disappointed, wondering how I was going to break the news to the boys. They were so confident that certainly one of the tracks was a hit. Now it seemed like the end of the road. Then I remembered another mantra my mentor often used to say to me: "It's not what happens to you that matters but how you respond to what happens to you". I decided right there and then that this was not going to be the end of the road for us and the project. I still believed in the boys and their music and I also knew that where there's a will, there's a way. I just had to find it.

I returned to the office and all the members of the team, together with the boys, were waiting for me. I broke the disappointing news but then told them that it was not over. I declared that I believed in the boys and I would sign them to my label and raise the money somehow so that we could press up some CDs and start promoting and selling our product ourselves. Everyone was smiling again, except me— I hadn't a clue at that precise moment in time where I was going to get the money from to produce the CDs, as well as come up with a marketing budget. We made a verbal agreement that the boys would sign the publishing rights to the tracks to my company in return for my investment.

It would take a couple of weeks to draw up the contract; however, we were a unit and so I quickly set about working out a plan to raise the cash needed. I created a "cause", a thought seed, "where there's a will there's a way". I kept reciting this to myself over and over.

A couple of weeks later, an amazing opportunity was presented to me.

Lucy, one of the members of my core team, was doing some freelance work at MTV Base and was working on the "World Aids Concert" which was being staged in South Africa that year and she had created an opportunity for one of the tracks from the EP to be used during the live broadcast to an audience of almost 2 billion. Everyone was very, very excited. I told Lucy that I had a gentleman's agreement with "Roots Conquest". I stated that the contracts were being drawn up by my lawyers and reminded her that the boys were about peace, love, integrity and consciousness. With this assurance, she in turn confirmed with her boss at MTV that we had an agreement in principle and that we'd have a signed copy faxed to him before the live broadcast, although it was going to be real tight.

The following Monday, work began in haste to tie up the publishing contracts and press up CDs, as I had now raised some funds with which we could get our first box of CDs. I pulled out all the stops and lined everything up. Lucy flew back from South Africa that Friday where she had already started working with the MTV Team on the forthcoming event. We met up and checked that everything was in place regarding the publishing and mastering of the tracks. It was a full on weekend as we were also staging the "Final" for the "Urban Voice 2003" Talent competition, which was supported by our first Ambassador, a new rising star called "Ms Dynamite". It was a lot of hard work, but great fun as this was what I loved doing. The show was a great success.

Lucy was on a plane back to South Africa two days later and I assured her that contracts would be signed and faxed over by the end of the week when the boys were scheduled to meet at my office to sign.

That week seemed to be one of the longest weeks ever. I spoke daily with both Lucy and the boys. Finally the day came and as I waited for 6pm to arrive, which was the time the boys were scheduled to meet with me, I wondered how what would take place over the next few minutes would impact the boys' career. Their music was soon to be exposed to a potential audience of 2 billion people, a very large audience.

There was a knock at the door. I said "Come in" and the boys entered. I greeted them with a beaming smile as I asked them to take a seat; however, I couldn't help noticing a slight tension on their faces. I asked them what was wrong. They replied that they didn't want to sign the contract. It was like a silent bomb went off.

We sat in silence for a few seconds as I tried to digest what had just been said. I reminded the boys of our agreement and the financial commitment that had been invested into the project and that there were people on the other side of the world waiting for this agreement, no less to talk of the golden opportunity that lay before them. The phone rang. It was Lucy in South Africa asking what was happening and that we had 60 minutes to send the signed document through by fax or they would have to line up other material. I persisted to make the boys see sense, but they were not prepared to sign, making all kinds of excuses. It was a long hour. Finally I got a call from Lucy saying we had run out of time.

I sat back in my chair, looking at the boys. I told them that their actions (cause) this night would have a damaging effect on their career for years to come. They probably would never get an opportunity like this again and with that I asked them to leave my office. I think that as soon as they closed the door behind them as they left my office they began to realise the (effects) of their actions

The effect of their decision taken on that night caused a meltdown of our relationship and that of my team towards them. In fact, I had to forbid some from taking matters to the street—I'm sure you get my drift. The craziest thing was that a couple of weeks later, the contract that was issued was signed, but of course by then the golden opportunity had gone. Things were never quite the same again as they had demonstrated to both my team and I that they had a lack of congruency in their words, music and lifestyle. We no longer had faith in them.

This story illustrates negatively the power of cause and effect where one action (cause) can in one sweep have a devastating impact (effect) that spans both time and space. In an instant, the actions taken that night had an effect on the other side of the planet.

Acknowledging this principle and the realization that you can initiate causes through your words, deeds, actions and even thoughts illustrates you posses the ability to initiate causes that can have a rippling effect. I don't know what the boys were thinking, but one thing is for sure—they were not thinking and focused on the desired effect. Some of the younger members in my team wanted to take matters into their own hands, saying "That's money that they just threw away—our money". But knowing this principle meant knowing that if I sanctioned this response I would be creating another cause which would set off another series of effects, and this would not end pretty at all. As I did not want to create those outcomes, as difficult as it was, I had to therefore exercise restraint over my boys.

It was a very dark period for us all.

Chapter 4

Principle 2:
The Power of Love

LOVE what *YOU* do and *DO* what *YOU* love
You'll never do a day's work again!

LOVE + INTELLIGENCE = CREATIVITY.

The absence of LOVE in one's life is stagnation and decay. Embracing and exploring this creativity brings with it a quiet confidence, a knowing that I CAN FIND A WAY. I WILL DO THIS.

Have you noticed that in recent years, many established organisations, agencies and systems that have served us for decades and even longer seem all of a sudden to be crumbling? For example, look at our healthcare system that has served us since being set up back in 1948. Recently, there has been widespread discussions and debates that suggest that it can no longer adequately support today's demands on it and that it will crumble if radical changes are not made and made fast. Similarly, throughout the elderly care system, we increasingly hear through the national news of failing care homes where elderly patients have been abused by individuals working within organisations which were set up to supposedly care for our elderly.

This has resulted in many organisations being investigated to discover what were the failings and in some cases resulting in the shutting down of the facility all together. Within the youth service, increasingly we are hearing more and more stories through the media of cases where vulnerable young people are being failed by the very agencies that are there to protect them. Each time we are told that lessons have been learnt and then a new case emerges. How many appalling cases have appeared on the news since the "baby P" case rocked the nation?

If we turn to our education system throughout primary, secondary and particularly further and higher education, there are massive problems. Tens of thousands of young people are leaving university with degrees and debts in some cases in excess of £50,000 incurred through young people paying for degrees which they took out believing that investing in the degree would create better opportunities for them to get better jobs. Better jobs it was thought would mean more income, which in turn would mean people could pay off their student loan and enjoy a good lifestyle and success, the ultimate goal. The reality for many however is low paying jobs, which often have no relationship with the degree they studied for.

This problem of youth unemployment is not just restricted to the UK. In a recent study conducted in the African country of Nigeria, almost 30 million young people are reported to be unemployed, despite a significant amount holding more than 1 degree. That's almost half the population of the UK. The global figure is estimated to be around 75 million. All these examples illustrate that the old ways of doing things no longer seem to be as effective or even working. I believe we need a new approach to dealing with unemployment, particularly youth unemployment. If you are seeking a job, this requires you to not just seek a job for the sake of simply having or doing your job, but rather know very clearly what you have to bring to the table. That is to say if you love what you do, and do what you love when you go to any interview, the interviewer will quite literally feel your vibes and you will stand out. Don't just take my word for it, try it.

During my brief spell within the education system back in 2006, I had the opportunity to meet with many employers as part of my role at South Thames College based in South London. Part of my remit was to look at the gap between the billions spent in educating our young people and the seemingly lack of suitable young people available to take up key positions within companies. They called it the "skills gap".

I had been approached (notice like I stated earlier when you genuinely love what you do and are doing what you love, people notice and seek you out, not the other way round) by the head of the music department at the college and invited to apply for a job which entailed heading up a new and dynamic department which would be responsible for the forging of relationships with employers on the one hand, whilst on the other hand demonstrating best practice to other colleges within the creative industries across the country. I applied, as I was very keen to explore the role that Further Education played in supporting the dreams and aspirations of young people. I got the job.

I settled in quite quickly, why wouldn't I? I was getting paid a lot to do what I loved to do. I was surrounded by young people who were passionate about music like I was and who I could empower and inspire.

One of the first things I noticed was the many Apple Mac computers in the music department. I discovered that a large budget had been set aside to purchase a whole lot more. I asked my team, including my line manager, if Apple had ever been approached in terms of sponsorship. I was told that was not a possibility. I asked why not. I didn't get a coherent answer. Around the same time that I was enjoying my new role at the college, I was also overseeing activities over at Urban Voice. Many months earlier, I had been approached by the Prince's Trust to advise them on what became known as the biggest Urban Music Festival at the time, a 2-day event which featured the likes of Jay-Z, Alicia Keys, Lemar, Dizzie Rascal and a host of other acts. The Prince's Trust were planning to stage the festival again in 2005 and I saw an opportunity to bring my department at the college into the event. As a result, the college was the only education establishment to take part in the 2005 festival, providing a large learning suite to attendees which was kitted out with Apple Macs, laptops, and iPods, as well as Apple specialist trainers on hand to help people as they experimented with using the equipment as well as delivering master classes. I had achieved what was said to be impossible and I felt real good. That's what happens when you are doing what you love and loving what you do, nothing is impossible.

My team and I continued to work hard and after a few months the department was awarded the kite mark of Centre of Vocational Excellence (CoVE). This was a big deal because we now became part of a major project with a budget of 200 million pounds distributed amongst 400 CoVE colleges across the UK (£500k per college), with each college acting as a beacon of excellence, high standards and best practices. My title was Head of CoVE for Music Technology.

One of my next assignments was to meet with various employers to get their take on how to address the issue of the "skills gap". After the successful Urban Music Festival event with Apple, I decided that Apple was an employer I wanted to meet with to get their take on this subject. It turned out to be one of the most significant meetings I held during my period in this role. The meeting was with the head of Apple UK, Mark Rogers. The year was 2005. During that meeting, I gained an insight into the way the commercial sector viewed the education system and its supply of a skilled and job-ready workforce or not as the case may be.

The driver pulled up outside the Apple Headquarters and I made my way to reception. After a short wait, I was escorted to his office. We shook hands and as we sat down he thanked me for taking the time to come and meet and discuss with him some of the issues surrounding youth employment within his sector. Apparently, hardly anyone from the educational sector had engaged with him to get his thoughts and views. As he spoke, I got the impression that he saw the education system, as somewhat institutionalised as it was used to receiving its regular funding from government and that the "Further Education" sector rarely seemed to engage with employers such as himself to understand some of the issues commercial companies were facing around the lack of young people with the right skill set who were ready for employment. (Have things improved since then? I sincerely hope so). Then he proceeded to ask me a very interesting question, which was one of those defining moments that stay with you.

He illustrated to me the importance of what I call "the LOVE Factor" in one's work. Love produces passion and a person who brings their passion to work with them everyday is a force to be reckoned with.

The question he posed and I am paraphrasing went something like this:

If two young people were presented to me for interviews with the aim of me hiring one of them, one was a graduate with a degree in computing or something similar and the other was a kid perhaps at college who had little more than soft skills (a term I was beginning to hear increasingly amongst employers which basically meant skills like a good attitude, desire to work, good people and communications skills, that kind of stuff) coupled with a love and passion for computers, which could be demonstrated by things they had had done, he asked me who do you think I would chose and how do you think I would make that choice?

His answer blew me away.

He said the guy without the degree! In my mind I thought, *what did you just say!* He saw my perplexed expression, so he went on to explain that in his business, things were moving at such speed and pace that often times they found that the guy coming out of University, although holding a degree, often was not up to date with the latest technology. The other guy, on the other hand, who was simply so passionate about computers although lacking in academic qualification often made up for this with raw passion and his love for all things to do with computers and computing.

This often translated in not only them being current with technology, but often yielded an ability to come at their work with an openness to learn, adaptability and creativity that often the guy with the university degree did not posses. This type of person could be trained up to be an asset within the company.

I was like WOW! I was hearing from the head of the UK branch of one of the most successful companies and brands on the planet the importance of making your "passion your work and your work your passion".

I had an instant paradigm shift—It was not just that there was a scarcity of jobs, but also a wealth of new and exciting opportunities which required not merely workers, but people who were seeking to work for a company in an area of work that they cared about, thus allowing them to engage and bring their passion to work each and every day.

When you find such a role within a company, it is not just a job; it is how you creatively express who and what you are. Imagine the idea that you could discover what you were passionate about and get paid for doing just that, your passion. I began thinking of the idea "turning your passion In2 profits". Now how cool is that! *Now that's what the education system should be teaching our youth*, I thought. This was the new world being presented, a world where the dominant question being asked is what meaningful contribution can you make, what problem can you help a company or others solve? This was the vision of the new world.

I left the meeting with three dominant words on my mind. LOVE, PASSION and CREATIVITY. The importance of Love, passion and creativity within the workplace was undeniable.

Then I thought, but what if a young person has not discovered their passion, then what? Which schools, colleges or Universities teach you how to identify and nurture your passion or passions? Did the education establishment, or for that matter our society as a whole, understand, embrace, celebrate and foster the spirit of creativity, allowing and encouraging individuals to explore and identify what they were passionate about and love doing? I was struggling to find any evidence of this.

My mentor and life itself has helped me realise that if you Love to give as a "conscious giver", it is almost impossible that your life will not resemble that of a successful person. By conscious giver, I mean someone who is always looking for opportunities to "invest" in others because they love to give.

The GPS System

Whatever you do, do not underestimate the power of Love; it can cause you to move mountains.

Back in 1992 when my children were both very small, both under 7, my relationship with their mother hit the rocks and I soon found myself homeless, having lost virtually all my worldly possessions including access to my children. That was more than 20 years ago and most definitely one of my darkest periods. However, I share this with you not that you might feel sorry for me, but rather to share one of the greatest lessons I have ever learnt, even though I did not realise it at the time.

You see, in that space, I found myself re-evaluating my life, my purpose and above all what was most important to me. I soon came to realise that my children literally meant the world to me. I loved them dearly and this enforced separation brought this home to me. So despite the advice given to me with good intention by friends and family to move on and concentrate on my career (I had recently completed my degree in Architecture), I decided to focus on where my love was. Fuelled by that love,

I spent the next 4 years battling through the British court system to try and gain access and then custody of my children, as their mother preferred for them to live separately, one with her and one with me. Eventually I would gain full custody of them both. But that journey changed everything for me. For that was how I came to realise and learn that children are literally shaped by "us the adults" and more often than not we dump our emotional and psychological "garbage" on them and then look surprised when many of them go AWOL during their teens.

Inspired by my mentor's suggestion (a good mentor never tells you what to do; they merely suggest) to grow empowered children as opposed to simply raising kids — there is a profound difference as you will soon discover — I slowly began to realise that these two children would soon become my teachers through which I would learn some of my greatest life lessons.

Over time, I discovered many things through my relationship with them, but none more powerful than the realisation that as parents our main duty and responsibility is to love our children. We should not see our children as things we posses or own, rather, that we are merely custodians and in the time you have together in those early years a parent's role is to nurture their child. I believe there is nothing that will pay more dividends in ways you cannot fathom than teaching your child or children how to explore their passions through identifying what they love and then creatively explore how to turn that passion into profits.

By the time both my children had reached the aged of 13, they had changed from ordinary kids to extraordinary children, simply because they had identified what they loved doing and were both in hot pursuit.

It was amazing to watch Jaie with her passion for singing and Joshua with his passion for athletics and business. Within a few years, we would be having conversations around the dinner table where they would be expressing their views to me that the UK was not doing enough to support young entrepreneurship and so they would be looking outside the UK in their pursuit of their success. To my surprise, in just a few years, so said so done — they were gone. Jaie went to Nigeria pursing her singing career after being offered a major recording contract there, which took her career to international status and new heights. During the first six months I recall on one occasion she called me saying, "Dad I wake up during the night sometimes and pinch myself to see if this is real or if I am dreaming".

Joshua went to USA as a result of getting into a scholarship program to study a degree in Business and marketing, we flew out a few days after his 20th birthday. Although they both kept me in the loop, what was amazing to watch was how they both created and orchestrated these situations totally by themselves. That's what I mean when I say "the power of Love". When you are doing or pursuing what you love, you become unstoppable and if on that journey you share your passion as a gift with those around you, you will also be valued very highly.

The meaning of life is to find your passion and the purpose of life is to give it away. – Pablo Picasso (*as a gift,* might I add)

It is mainly through watching my children, my students and mentees journey that this Grow Personal Success book, coaching workshops and programs have been put together so as to fast track you to your success. Take a few seconds to register on the http://www.growpersonalsuccess.com private members website and choose a Free bonus gift from a selection of offers. I have been blessed through having found my passion. My gift is to empower you that you might discover yours and live a fulfilled life through giving and sharing your passion as a gift.

If the job positions in our care-homes, youth service or schools were filled with people who had identified that this was their passion and they were coming to work bringing their passion to work every day, would these institutions be very different? I believe so. When you love what you do and are doing what you love, you walk and talk with a different vibe, a different energy; there's an aura around you and if one employer (Apple) can detect it, is it possible that all employers can, dare I say that all do detect it and are all actually looking for it? That's the question, or are some employers just looking for people who can do the job? The problem is most of us do not know what we are passionate about, what stirs up our emotions, what our gifts, talents and natural abilities are and there lies the problem. On the Grow Personal Success Coaching program, we take you through a process which helps you identify your natural, talents, gifts and abilities, which often translate as indicators pointing towards your passion.

In the old world, the focus was on getting a good education so you could get a good job and then have a job for life (less than 50 years ago, people actually believed this, how funny is that) so that you would have money for life and therefore be successful for life.

The reality is that was the old world. In the new world, success comes though knowing how you want to show up in the world and I mean that literally. When people Google your name on the internet or search for you on LinkedIn, do you even show up and if you do, do they see someone who appears to be all over the place pursuing one thing and then another, regularly changing their job? Or do they see someone who has a constant theme running through what they are doing? When you do not know what you want to be, what you want to do and what you want to have, a lack of this constant theme is often the result.

So here's a question for you: are you looking to work your passion, does your current job role or the job role you are seeking allow you to do your passion or are you just looking to get paid? Notice the choice of words here — one illustrates a person whose focus is on giving what they have, what they love and what they are passionate about; the other illustrates a person wanting to get money for which they are willing to exchange some time, knowledge or skill. One provides a transactional experience; the other creates a transformational experience. One operates from a place of I have in abundance, both my passion and desire to do what I love and therefore I am wanting and willing to share and experience how my contribution makes a positive change; the other has a limited amount of time—168 hours per week to be precise—and skill set for which they simply seek to exchange to the highest bidder. Think about this for a little while.

Chapter 5

Principle 3:
The Law of the Mind

As a man Thinketh — Scarcity or abundance — Choose one.

A New World

The third principle — The law of the mind is made plain by the phrase "As a man Thinketh". This is based on the ancient wisdom that if you believe that you have (and we are not just talking money here) and give from this place of abundance, somehow through ways that cannot be predetermined, you receive more. However, if you believe you do not have anything or not enough (joy, peace, happiness, love, health, strength, etc.) even the little you have will be reduced. So the question is, do you realise or even know what you have?

During the late 90's, my mentor told me about the new age that was dawning. He spoke about a time to come, which he called the "Information age", where man's thirst for knowledge would intensify. In this new world, people would not be satisfied with just doing a job. Unbeknown as to why, many people would come to experience a deep restlessness, coupled with a deeper need to find fulfilment, a meaning, a purpose, a cause, a reason for being. In this new world, the sharing of knowledge and information towards this end would explode and become big business. I remembered thinking, *I can't see that happening.* However, today I can see evidence of this throughout the entire globe.

We are at a new frontier in the journey of human civilisation and our mind holds the key to many a breakthrough in this next evolution of mankind. The mind holds within it so many hidden treasures, so much so that on the 7th October 2013, you may have heard that scientists were awarded 1 billion pounds of funding to carry out studies, research, tests and explorations into this area. Here is a link to the direct site for more information: http://www.bbc.co.uk/news/health-24428162.

So here's another question. What company or organisation would invest 1 billion pounds into something without a certainty or at least being pretty confident that such an investment would yield a return greater than the original investment made? Think about that for a moment; a billion pound investment project into the unknown, or is it? I predict the next 20 years are going to produce things that will literally boggle the minds of today.

A paradigm shift is occurring which will cause us to change the way we currently see the world. Fortunately, believe it or not, if you're under 25, this will be quite easy for you to adjust to as you have already been experiencing this new world forming for a significant period during your formative years. For you, any necessary adaptation to this new paradigm is not so difficult; in fact, for you it's normal. For the rest of us, however, we must prepare ourselves for change, as challenging as it may be, and embrace this change, educating ourselves through the learning of new things or we'll simply get left behind, quite literally!

Roger Bannister, the first athlete to run a mile in under 4 minutes proved this. He proved that the old thinking, views and ways of doing things will eventually fall and be replaced by a better, more efficient, effective way, brought to us by people whose minds see only an abundance of new possibilities in this the new world.

Imagine for a moment the mindset that Roger Bannister must have had to achieve what he achieved. Every single indicator around him pointed to the fact that to run a mile in under 4 minutes was impossible, but he focused on the belief that it was possible, excluding everything else and then most amazing of all, took action, based on this belief and mindset, subjecting himself to rigorous daily discipline through training with the sole intention of achieving the impossible.

Think about this for a moment. If I gave you a task to complete that you considered impossible, you would look at me as if I were crazy and probably say something like "You must be mad, I am not doing that, it's impossible!" Yet Roger Bannister did precisely the opposite of what most of us would do, almost as if he had some kind of insight no one else had, that the seemingly impossible was in fact possible.

What is even stranger about Roger Bannister's achievement is what happened within the next 12 months after he smashed the 4-minute mile barrier. Within the next 12 months, that which had never been achieved before was suddenly achieved by scores of people throughout the country. In the following few years, hundreds would go on to run a mile with a time of under 4 minutes. Today, even college students are achieving these same times. How come?

The power of belief

This illustration emphatically demonstrates the fact that what we believe holds the key to what we can achieve and what we ultimately experience in our life. The news of Roger's achievement travelled across the country. The fact that someone had actually done it, smashed the 4-minute mile, meant that everyone experienced a instant paradigm shift, everyone was forced to accept it, like it or not, that the previously considered impossible was in fact POSSIBLE.

Now the moment this was whole-heartedly embraced, that is to say people truly believing this with their hearts as well as their minds due to real tangible irrefutable evidence, it immediately became a POSSIBILITY for those believers too.

My question to you is what do you believe is possible or impossible for you? I don't just want you to think it; I want you to write it down and read it out aloud to yourself. Like all other GPS exercises, you will find this is not as simple as it seems, if you keep it real. For whatever you believe deeply, your mind holds this for you and begins to operate almost like an incubator — the inner space where you create the "cause" where if outer conditions become or are made to be conducive, that which you hold in your mind (incubator) soon takes form to emerge as your experience, as your reality and your true life experience.

We Are One

We are all connected through one mind consciousness.

Old-school singer/songwriter Frankie Beverley wrote and sang a song that was a great hit and a classic called "We are one" http://youtu.be/A2SfKTS-g8c and Roger Bannister's story proves it. We are all connected through a universal mind consciousness, as my mentor once shared with me, and Roger's story illustrates this. The moment he achieved the seemingly impossible, we — all of humanity — benefited because it became believable, achievable and possible for the rest of us. As a result, those who really wanted to simply accessed this new reality through tapping into that mindset, that state of consciousness as held by Roger Bannister, and it instantly became a possibility for them too. Studying Roger's discipline, and physical training, diet and belief would also further increase the probability for success. By the same token, once you are clear of what you want to achieve in your life, one way in which you can make massive strides toward that desired objective is by finding out about people who have achieved that which you desire. In short, import their mindset into yours. Read, study, research what they went through to get to that position, whether that be a position of wealth, fame, a dream career, marriage, whatever you seek for your life. But you must first believe it to be possible, adopting the abundance mindset that it is possible. You must have an abundant mindset that every problem has millions of solutions and you are required to be "solution oriented", in fact "solution focused". You only need to identify one solution, choose it by zooming in on it, and then take action.

This reminds me of a story that occurred many years ago which amusingly illustrates the idea of being solution focused. The idea of always being solution focused was something I had introduced to my children before they hit their teens. One Saturday evening, I was hanging out in my daughter's room and we were just chatting. Jaie was doing her hair whilst Josh was lying on her bed flicking through a magazine as we chatted about nothing in particular. Then Josh introduced the subject of his school and his teachers, he had been quite upset for a number of days because at school some teachers were putting pressure on him. You see, Josh was at that age (13) where young people are beginning to become aware of their self-image and he was into wearing his hair in cane rows (plaiting of the hair in rows). He had spent months growing his hair to achieve this style and now he was being told by his teacher that he had to shave it all off as it was not acceptable at the school. He was upset and angry stating that other boys were able to wear their hair long and in various styles.

He felt it was not fair as he really did not want to cut his hair, but his teacher had given him an ultimatum — shave the hair or be suspended.

As he shared his dilemma, he suddenly sat up on the bed and shrieked, "I've got it, I've got it" and with that he dashed out of the room leaving both his sister and I perplexed, as he did not reply to our question "got what". I was to find out days later his ingenious solution. Apparently he had returned a few hours later with a lady's wig and then explained his idea to his sister, who excitedly joined the plot. She took the wig and trimmed it down to a reasonable size. Josh then took the wig and every day for the next 3 months went to school with his wig in his bag. Upon getting to within 100 yards of the school gate, he then took the wig out of the bag and put it on his head. Then he went into school sporting his new hairdo. It was a perfect solution. After school he would walk out the school gates and then once 100 yards away from the school gate, he would whip his wig off put it back in his school bag and sport his cane rows.

His teachers were none the wiser and he got to keep his hair in cane rows. It was hilarious; even a couple of the other boys copied the trick.

The teachers eventually did find out months later, but they found his solution focused attitude so funny that it won him their respect and became a joke at school. The teachers came to realise that hairstyles was not what school was about. Joshua eventually outgrew the cane row phase and he cut his hair.

Take action based on the clarity of the desired goal in mind and more importantly why that goal is so important to you and why that goal must be achieved is crucial. Simply put, always ensure that you have set a very clear intention for the desired objective, in other words a very clear reason why this goal must be achieved.

Question: How many people live their lives setting clear intentions on a regular or even daily basis?

Intention Deficiency Syndrome

My friend Rev. Michael Beckwith introduced me to this term. He actually coined the phrase. He said the world was full of people suffering from this condition. It simply describes that state of mind many people operate from on a daily basis. We have come to see and are now beginning to realise the power that the mind holds. Scientists say we currently use less than 10% of our brain, wherein lies our mind. We have also come to acknowledge the power of belief. However, if your thoughts and beliefs are devoid of a clear intent, then much goes to waste.

I met Michael for the first time a few years ago (August 2010 to be precise) when I travelled to Ghana to attend an event celebrating my mentor's 35th anniversary of his mission and work. Michael was the founder and leader of a worldwide spiritual centre called Agape based in Los Angeles. He had a massive following with 5,000 attendees regularly attending one of the many services held on a Sunday at their church. It was a very vibrant "New thought" church, attracting lots of new and established creatives and celebrity folk such as film directors, musicians, actors like Eddie Murphy, singers like the legendary Chaka Khan and many more. Rev. Michael had also come for the celebration because to my surprise he also knew my mentor. Agape had recently gone through a massive surge in attendance because Rev. Michael had participated in a DVD film called *The Secret* which became a massive hit for its creator and producer Rhonda Burn after she made it on to *The Oprah Show*. It was that big!

I had already come across *The Secret*. I had watched the video back in the UK and even incorporated elements of it into some of my lesson plans to provoke discussion with some of my students who were on our personal development programme. So it was an honour to meet the man in person and also to find out that we shared a mutual friend, as his relationship with my mentor spanned some 15 years.

As we talked one afternoon, he shared with me his Intention Deficiency Syndrome theory. He pointed out that simply being aware of this sickness and guarding against it on a daily basis would massively improve the quality and effectiveness of one's life. (So if success is what you truly seek, then this must—and I repeat must—be your daily habit.) Intention Deficiency Syndrome describes a state of mind where there is a lack of belief in one's own ability to establish something. He shared that setting a clear intention before the start of each and every day brought clarity and focus to that day; it is by default a declaration you make to yourself that the intention set is possible. Through this process, this in turn increases the "causes" in one's daily activities as well as increases your daily productivity significantly simply because there is an intention held in mind regarding the priorities of that particular day. As we now know, intentions come from a far deeper place within us than the source of mere goal setting. A goal for the day is something you plan to do and may or may not accomplish or even start within the time frame specified that day. An intention for the day, however, is much more important and must be established that day and is usually held in mind until accomplished. You have a clear reason as to why the intention has to be established that day (or re-established, if it is an intention carried over from the previous day).

For example, imagine you have been nursing a throbbing toothache all week and you phoned your dentist and by some miracle they were able to make you an appointment for the very next day because the dentist is away on holiday for a week after that. When you wake the next day, you will have a very clear intent that you will make it to that dentist on time no matter what. It is not some flimsy goal that you may get around to; it is your dominant thought all day. Regardless of your other tasks, chores, activities and whatever else you may be doing that day, your intention is to make that appointment and nothing or no one will be allowed to get in the way. **Why?** Because the pain is unbearable and seeing the dentist is the only chance you have of getting rid of the pain. That is a clear intention, you are certain and there is absolutely no doubt or confusion about your intent, because you have a clear **why**.

Decide right here and right now never to suffer from the Intention Deficiency Syndrome, start each day, and move through the day holding clear definite intentions. Why not set an intention for the week, month or year.

When you have discovered your purpose there is an intention for your life.

Confusion is created through a lack of clarity

Let me share with you a technique for dissolving confusion from your life. Possessing and maintaining clarity of the "why" behind any intention dissolves any confusion you may have had surrounding that thing. Don't just take my word for it test—it out for yourself. Pick something, anything, which has been causing you some unsettledness because you have been somewhat confused as to whether you should or should not pursue this thing or course of action. Then simply ask yourself the question "Is there an intention behind this thing or issue?" If so, ask yourself the question "What is it?" Once clear about what the intention is, then line it up with our agreed definition of success—Is it something that you enjoy doing, does it honour you and lastly is it positive, does it promote life? If you have three yeses as your answers, then right there you have identified your intention and you can proceed. If you have a "no" amongst your answers, you'd probably be wise not to proceed without asking yourself some more questions because you don't have the clear "why" as to why you should proceed. Job done! No more confusion. Three yeses are the only basis for taking action, which supports the action based on a solid foundation from deep within you, because you know why this is so important to you. Have you noticed the state of confusion dissolving already?

So there we have it, a formula for dissolving confusion, which is often responsible for clouding our vision of what personal success looks like for us. Establish lots of daily intentions where your life is concerned and thus dissolve confusion from different areas of your life; the result will be increased clarity, little by little each day as to the direction your GPS should be taking you.

The GPS System coaching programme helps establish or re-affirm a clearer sense of intentions within a short period of time and this is why students often experience rapid progress, clarity and breakthroughs.

Register at http://www.growpersonalsuccess.com to receive newsletter and further info on courses some of which will be 100% Free, others heavily discounted (members only) through funding received by Urban Voice UK my charitable organisation.

Always remember:

You can't experience what you can't conceive Therefore conceive, believe and achieve.

If it's conceivable, it's believable. If it's believable, it's possible. If it's possible, it's achievable. And if it's achievable, YOU can attain it if you establish your intention.

If you are a parent or teacher reading this book, may I suggest that the sooner you can present this formula to your young ones, the better. Do not think that they are too young to grasp these ideas and concepts; they are not. Often times that is the problem; we adults think that young ones can't grasp things, so we make a decision (in our infinite wisdom) not to present to them. Remember my chess game experiment with my son at 3? Test this intention exercise with your young one and note the results.

Back in October 2010, I had the good fortune of teaching one of our personal Empowerment programmes to a small group of children aged 11-13 at a school called Battersea Park in South London. I would like to further illustrate the law of "as a man Thinketh" through the encounter I had with a little boy in that group.

It was 9:00 am in the morning and I was already set up, eager and excited to engage with my 12 new students who were enrolled in the Success Genius personal development programme. It was a programme that had been entrusted to me by my mentor after one of our many conversations about how to inspire and promote high aspirations amongst young people this age. I had adapted the programme through introducing some basic tweaks.

The students began to tumble through the door. "Morning Sir!" one shouted as he dumped his school bag on the desk. "Morning", I replied. "Where are the rest of the students?" I asked him. "I don't know sir", was his response. "Would you like me to go check at the office?" I didn't have a chance to respond. The door opened and the head of year appeared with 8 young people behind her. "Sorry we're a little late", she said as the young people filed past her. "I should have 12 for you, but I could only find 8 this morning. Can you begin with this group and I'll go find the rest of them." I indicated that was fine. Once everyone was settled, I introduced myself and we began our session with introductions about me and the Success Genius Programme.

Why I will never forget this group is because halfway through the session, I asked the students to write down a list of at least 10 things that they were good at. I explained that at the end of the exercise, everyone was going to read their list to the rest of the class. I told them that I would give them a few minutes and with that they buried their heads and began to write, except this one little boy. He just stared at the blank sheet of paper. He looked very timid and withdrawn and I could tell by the way he carried himself that he lacked confidence. I observed him.

When the time was up, I invited the students to share the contents of their list and they did. Each had a list that ranged from 5 – 10 things, except this little boy. When it came to his turn he sheepishly said, "I could not think of anything that I am good at sir", feeling very sorry for himself. This was my opportunity. "Really?" I said in disbelief. Then his friend sitting next to him nudged him in that boisterous way that young boys do. "Come on man, what's wrong with you, don't you fix all our bikes whenever we got a problem with them?" he said. "Oh yeah", he softly responded. I smiled at him and said, "So you are good at something, so why not write that down". He gave a brief smile and wrote on the sheet of paper. I gave them all homework to think about other things they were good at, as they would be extending their list the following week.

As I closed the door behind the last student as they hurried to their next lesson, I smiled to myself as I thought about the little boy. I thought to myself, *something transformational may have just taken place in a young boy's life.* I couldn't wait till next week.

The following week, I stood by the door eagerly waiting for my group to appear. As the lesson bell sounded, the door burst open and in they filed. "Where is Adrian?" I asked. Adrian was the name of my little shy guy. Just as I spoke he walked through the door. "Morning sir", he smiled.

We sat down and began our lesson. I explained we would be continuing from the work started last week and that I wanted them to extend their lists. The lists came out and they got to work. When it came round to sharing, everyone had been able to add significantly, including Adrian whose list now consisted of 10 things. This for me was amazing because in 1 week a young boy who did not believe in himself and didn't believe he had any value was transformed into a young boy who was beginning to now see his value and increasingly so.

Here are a few letters I received from parents of children in the Success Genius Programme, along with the student feedback of what they thought about the programme once it had concluded. For confidentiality, I have deliberately left out their names.

Success Genius Programme Spring 2011

Dear Tony,

I would like to express my gratitude and appreciation for my son's improvement since attending the Success Genius classes. My son has changed his attitude at home and is much calmer and more focused and has more of a smile rather than a frown on his face. He has more direction, feels a better sense of worth and really believes in himself a lot more than before. That belief is one of "I Can

Achieve and Be The Best Me". He is also much more focused on his future and direction his life is going and is aware that only he is ultimately responsible for the direction and choices he makes — including the outcome or end result of actions — and simply more aware of the possible consequences from his attitude and behaviour.

He has told me he is now much more focused at school and is determined to keep the positive changes growing. It doesn't happen overnight, but he now has small seeds planted within him to aid his growth from a young boy into adolescence and adulthood.

I feel these changes have come about as a result of direct input from you via the skills and mental challenging my son went through whilst attending these classes. My son's imagination seems to have woken up to all the possible realities he could achieve now and in the future just by being the "best" him that he can be.

Dear Tony,

Just a short letter to give you some feedback since my son has been attending your course.

He has really looked forward to going every week and has always been happy and in a good mood when returning home.

I have found that my son will listen more when something is explained to him and will ask questions about things that he does not understand, which he did not do before. When asking certain questions about things, they seem to be more direct rather than muddled and not straight to the point. I think he now feels more confident talking about certain things rather than keeping them to himself and if he's not sure, he will ask for an explanation.

I would like to thank you for your time and effort improving the above problems stated.

Here are the student survey questions used to gather feedback and some feedback comments from some of the children on the impact the programme had on them.

Student Survey

Question 1: How much have you learnt that you are able to apply at your school life or everyday life?

Answer: In School life – In my school life I've been able to be punctual due to the fact that it helps me gain more information in all my lessons.

Answer: In Everyday life – Be focused on what I really love doing. Practice on what I love the most outside of school.

Answer: In Everyday life – I am more aware of what comes to me. Learnt to go to places on time

Answer: In School life – Working harder in subjects that interest me.

Answer: In Everyday life - Working on myself daily to improve.

Answer: In Everyday life – To believe in yourself.

❖ 75% of students in their feedback said that they had found the programme very helpful. The remaining student found it helpful. Not one student said they did not find the programme useful. Things that all the students have in common are that they all have learnt a valuable lesson, particularly around punctuality and being focused and more aware of what they are currently doing in their life.

❖ Not one student left the programme without taking something away. Many asked why such a programme was not part of their everyday schooling.

Anthony Abiola Dada

PROJECTyourTALENT 4Business

Anurah was the winner of our PROJECTyourTALENT 4Business competition. He was a bright, talented and hard working young man who is destined to be successful; however, read in his own words how a mindset of scarcity as opposed to abundance nearly lost him the prize.

I am a young, extremely focused, dedicated and driven individual who has grown up with a very independent lifestyle. This has led me to become very opportunistic in life and to demonstrable success within studying electrical installation and engineering, music technology, sports fitness, tae kwon do competitions, and starting my own business with the help of The Prince's Trust.

So using this high energy that I have, I attended exhibitions such as the business show to explore avenues to build my business. In doing this I met Serah, a director at Urban Voice UK at the small business show at the Excel Centre in London in May 2013. Serah told me about a programme run by the Urban Voice founder Tony Biola called Growing Personal Success (GPS).

I explained my idea of starting up my business to her. "My Product helps employees who work in the exchange service via sanitary bins, to do their jobs more effectively because it allows the employee to carry the sanitary bins using a tool (my product) rather than their finger tips which can result in muscle strain. The Product was a commercial tool capable of carrying multiple sanitary bins by hand.

I was not sure about joining the Urban Voice UK membership scheme as I did not have any money or work that provided me with an income, but as I have an open mind, I attended the Launch of the PROJECTyourTALENT 4Business competition in Wandsworth cinema, where I learnt about what Urban Voice UK had to offer through this competition.

I then left the event thinking that the organisation had a good business mission which is to empower young adults to help them achieve their dream or realise their strengths and weaknesses so as to become successful personally and professionally with the right mindset.

A week later or so, Tony Biola gave me a call and explained in more detail the GPS programme scheme and its benefits as I had expressed an interest. I then explained to Tony that I did not have the money to pay for this service which at the time was £2,500. Tony then explained that I would get access to the course through him because he had noticed something special about me and as he spotted and invested in young talent, he was going to invest in me by sponsoring me through their scholarship programme. This meant that I did not have to worry about paying for the GPS programme. However, he suggested that I should sign up to the £10 a month membership scheme as the scholarship programme was awarded only to registered members. We then said goodbye. Reflecting on what was said, I realised that Tony asked me to sign up to the membership scheme, but as I did not feel that I had been listened to regarding the fact that I did not have any money, I decided that I could not join the GPS programme.

A few weeks went by and Tony decided to contact me and ask me why I had not been in touch, so I explained the misunderstanding and why I had decided I could not take up the offer. Tony told me my place on the GPS Programme was still available and to break the ice, I along with the other students in the course were invited to Tony's house for a sit-down meal with chicken and all the good stuff, whilst we talked and kept it real.

As we sat around the table and introduced ourselves, our passion and why we do what we do, I found myself sharing stories about my childhood. Tony talked about the fact that 50% of our mindset in terms of how we view the world based on our core beliefs is already set by the age of 5 and how we begin to deal with future situation as they begin to show up in our lives based on what he called "Pre-conditioned thinking", i.e., as soon as you see a situation similar to one you have previously experienced, Pre-conditioned thinking concludes that the outcome is going to be the same as before so you react immediately with that outcome in mind. That evening as we left Tony's place, we all looked forward to our individual one-to-one sessions with Tony.

Anurah's story provides a perfect illustration of the law of the mind at work and the power of "as a man Thinketh" as I will share, but not before I share a story of one of the other gentlemen present at the dinner table that same evening.

His name is Tuoyo (pronounced Ty-o). As we shared stories before dinner, he spoke of a recent incident that shocked him. He was out with some friends promoting their event through distributing leaflets and during the evening his friend turned round to him saying "bruv, you're a natural at this, how come I didn't know you were a promoter?" To which Tuoyo replied, "I'm not" and then he had a flashback. He shared with us that in that moment, he suddenly remembered that approximately 15 years before, when he was around 6 or 7, he worked for a period with me, my son and his uncle as part of my street team distributing leaflets. He said both he and his friend were in total shock as he shared it with him as they suddenly realised that due to those activities all those years ago, his mind had filed this activity as "this is something I know how to do" and he just switched into this mode of operation when invited. We were all flabbergasted.

Now back to Anurah. Our earlier conversations prior to our dinner date had resulted in our "knocking of heads", which was born out of his mantra "I don't have money", which I challenged as I saw issues of self-worth. As a result of this, Anurah's reaction to this was to cut off all communication. On noticing this, I made a conscious effort to reach out to him to ensure that he stayed on the programme..

Anurah went on to demonstrate this pattern once again through another incident, cutting all communication with Urban Voice and myself and eventually left the GPS programme. However I was well aware of this pattern by now and so together with Urban Voice director Serah, who has a fantastic way of working with challenged young people, together we supported him through this self-sabotaging tendency based on pre-conditioned thinking. Then something amazing happened — Anurah beat 9 finalists to win the NatWest PROJECTyourTALENT 4 Business competition, receiving over £17,000 worth of prizes in the form of business support, including the GPS Programme.

My team are planning the next PROJECTyourTALENT 4Business competition as well as PROJECTyourTALENT 4Music. Got to http://www.growpersonalsuccess.com If you would like to register for either of these exciting competitions.

If Anurah had let his pre-conditioned thinking rule, all ties and communications would have been cut and he would have missed out on realising this great achievement and all the publicity through the press which he went on to receive.

He later wrote to me saying,

I've learnt I need to gain clarity during conversations with people and listen more before deciding that I should cut the cloth, as I may miss out on opportunities that life has for me.

Life is 10% what happens to you, and 90% how you respond to it. Thank you Tony for staying connected with me no matter what.

Anurah has learnt many life lessons and much about himself throughout this process and is a young man full of determination and great potential.

Anurah's story clearly illustrates the law of the mind in action and the power it can exert on our future without us even being aware.

Chapter 6

Principle 4:
The Law of Gratitude

What you focus on grows – This is true for all things
(heart, mind and soul).

I find it amusing that young people have become a central piece to my life because as a young boy I always used to say that I was not going to have children until much later in life—little did I know what lay ahead of me. I could have chosen a very different path had I followed the path suggested by my advisors when my partner and I separated and I was denied access to the children. The advice I was given was to simply pursue my career and forget about the children for the time being as my ex-partner (as so many parents do) was using the children as weapons to create conflict, antagonism, and distress, for both me and the children, and so on the face of it this advice made sense. In other words, I was being advised to move my focus from the children because of the many barriers being constructed to thwart my attempts to maintain a healthy relationship with them.

At its darkest point, my son's mother and her family conspired and removed my son from the UK without my knowledge. So my advisors were giving me what looked like very logical, sound advice right?

However, that relationship break up and the mother's attempts to restrict my access to my children I now acknowledge was one of the best things that ever happened to me and I am eternally grateful for that experience as it made me question the importance and purpose of everything around me, including myself—yes even my very own existence and purpose— and that was how I discovered the "Y-Factor".

Unlike X-Factor, which is all about that hidden special ingredient or talent which only a select special few can detect in another, thus you might have the X-Factor and not even know it or see it yourself, the Y-Factor is at the complete opposite end of the spectrum. The Y-Factor is a simple process which ensures that anyone who applies this process will be provided with definite clarity about the subject to which it is applied. So much so, that I am convinced that this process can be used to gain a deeper sense of clarity on almost anything.

The Y-FACTOR Process

Through my break-up, I found myself asking what did I really want out life and WHY did I want it?

Asking these questions of myself set my life on the path of Growing Personal Success. You see, all of my family and friends were giving me advice based on their perspective of what my life currently looked like as far as they could see; more importantly, it was from THEIR PERSPECTIVE.

Although this was undoubtedly the darkest and most difficult period of my life, I have since realised that it was the best chain of events, as it forced me to wake up to the fact that ultimately only we can give real meaning to our lives and its purpose. If you fail to be responsible and make choices in your life and leave it to others to make those choices for you, be clear of what you are doing, for this is nothing short of surrendering your power. You are literally handing over your opportunity to Grow Personal Success to someone else for them to set your compass based on their view of who and what you are and most importantly, based on how they interpret the world.

This is a seriously dangerous place to be and you may have found yourself in a similar position where others are advising, telling or even dictating what you should be doing with your life based on what they believe is best for you. I have found this to be a most unhealthy practise adopted by many, including parents, friends and family, school teachers, college and university lecturers and the list goes on. I am not condemning these advisors as it often comes from a place of love, concern and care. However, they cannot always see your vision of a successful outcome. Knowing and putting this principle to work, I chose my own path. This was to make my children my focus, ensuring that I gave their mother no opportunity to deny them access to their father. It was hard, very hard. Eventually, albeit many years later, my vision of a successful outcome was realised; their mother freely gave me full and sole custody of our children. Without applying this principle, I believe, it just wouldn't have happened.

In raising our children, I taught them to apply the Y-Factor (respectfully ask why) as often as possible and if not happy or satisfied with the answer received, ask why until you got a satisfactory answer and if you did not get a reasonable answer, then bin it! Even if the answer came from me, their father, because in truth none of us knows all the answers. So my children were encouraged to ask as many questions as they needed to and that agreement meant that I had to think about my response when answering them and not just "react". Of course I messed up, loads of times. But when I messed up, I intentionally paid a price though giving them some kind of compensation, so that eventually they loved it when I messed up because their focus was on what price I would pay; it became a game.

Let me illustrate this point further—have you observed a young toddler interacting with its parent in one of those conversations that simply make you laugh. I had such an experience the other day. I was sitting on a park bench enjoying a rare sunny afternoon in September. Sat next to me was a mother and her toddler and next to them was a gentleman smoking a pipe. I hadn't seen someone smoking one of those for a very long time. The toddler asked, "Mummy what is that?" pointing to the pipe. The mother replied, "A pipe". The child then asked, "What's a pipe and what is he doing putting it in his mouth?" The mother replied, "He is smoking it". The toddler asked. "What is smoking it?" The mother replied, "It's when you burn some herbs and suck the smoke through a pipe because you like the smoke. This man likes smoking his pipe." The toddler asked again, "Why?" The mum answered, "I guess it's because he likes the taste." The toddler responded with yet another question, 'Why?" The mother replied, "Because he enjoys it". The toddler asked again, "Why?" By now the mother was totally exasperated, as she replied saying, "Darling, I really don't know why, shall we ask the man and let him tell us?" With that, she looked directly at the man who was now wearing a big grin on his face as she asked, "Why do you smoke that pipe?" I think you get the picture.

The Y-Factor process drills down until you get that clarity. Approached with an open mindset that this is an opportunity to gain understanding and receive information which will make you wiser, you are asking the why from a place of expectancy which should be followed by gratitude if you receive new knowledge, understanding or insights.

The GPS system ensures that you identify and grow personal success for yourself.

Now coming back to that question I asked myself — What did I really WANT out of life and WHY? I would like us to look at the 2 main words in those 2 questions for their meaning in relation to one's mindset.

The word "Want" — what does it mean? The dictionary suggests that the word want means a desire, a need, drawn from a place of lack or even poverty, aspire and to choose. Most of the synonyms I found associated with this word conveyed a sense of lack or negativity. The only words that were positive in any way were aspire and choose, but in the context that I had used the word this did not hold much positivity because I did not know what I wanted (at least initially) and this is the place that many young people find themselves at some point while growing up. How do we get the clarity on this?

I learnt from my mentor that many of us use the words "I want" from a position of lack, wanting far more than we actually need because this type of want is what I call an "acquisitions mindset" which is unconsciously creating spaces of lack or emptiness within us, with the idea and thinking that acquiring this thing or that will fill this void.

This requires us to adopt a new mindset to this one that is based on a sense of lack, which is actually a poverty mindset. In its place we are to adopt a mindset which is gratitude based. When we adopt this gratitude mindset, everything takes on a whole new meaning.

To experience the fullness of the principle of the Law of Gratitude, we must firstly redefine the word I want.

If your mindset is that the words "I want" brings to your awareness that you live in an absolutely benevolent and generous universe where everything has already been provided for you and you simply have to choose what you

their parents. As I BE-came increasingly aware of this love, I nurtured it within and it grew until it then overflowed into physical manifestation and expression towards my own children and then other people's children around me through the various events and activities I began staging, in an attempt to support them in my own little way.

Many young people on our personal development, mentoring and coaching programmes have often said that they think that parents should be made to attend such courses as well.

In fact, my own daughter on realising I was writing this book, requested that I insert a piece on this next topic.

Based on this law of gratitude, how many parents raise their children in the incorrect ordering of things as illustrated earlier, i.e., with the spirit of HAVING (possessing) their children first as opposed to BEING a good parent.

Based on this new understanding, if we act with the belief that we own our children like we own any of our other possessions, the point will come when the child will realise that this is not true. They will eventually come to the realization that they were not born to be possessed. Conflict will therefore ensue, and in this conflict if the parent focuses on that aspect which is causing the conflict within the relationship as opposed to focusing on that which they would like to see, the conflict will continue and rather than reduce will in fact grow, according to the law (what you focus on grows). Perhaps now you understand the principle behind why this so often is the experience of so many families. When you focus on the good, the positive and the virtues that you would like to see within the relationship and nurture these, you will find they will eventually overflow into physical manifestation and expression. I have found it is hard for a child or young person to rebuff acts of consistent and sustained kindness and love.

With this in mind, I would encourage every parent to apply this principle in your relationship with your child or children. Don't see them as your property; rather, see them as an asset to your life for which you are grateful and watch the fruits born from the principle unfold before your eyes. Give love and appreciation to your children — I have found these are the only gifts they truly seek.

Sadly, this is not the case in many homes where children are often used by a parent or both parents during disputes leading up to the separation as a pawn to score points, one against the other, or worse still used as a weapon to inflict pain on the other; for example, denying one parent access to the child. This approach does not, cannot and will never work. It will backfire on the instigator eventually and your child or children will also suffer long term as a result long. Display your gratitude, your love and your appreciation for your child, not your selfishness based on reacting to any hurt you may feel your partner may have caused you.

And if you know a family that has someone acting in this selfish kind of way, give them this book as a present so that they get an awakening when they get to this chapter.

We are dealing with Universal laws and principles here and it is my opinion that children should be seen as gifts for which we should be grateful. Engaging with our children from this place of gratitude produces more things to be grateful for in relation to one's children.

As a result, we in our society today have grown many broken children, with broken hearts or minds or both. I have found that what is required is early intervention and introducing love and appreciation into their relationships with others. If we as a society do not find ways to educate or set standards to which all parents can aspire in the art of good parenting, we all end up paying the price for those young people who go out into the community in a broken state. In this state, the person cannot function at their best.

In all our relationships with our family members, whether our parents, our children, our partners, our relatives, our friends, our classmates or our colleagues at work, let us show gratitude for the relationships. When we regularly remind ourselves that we do not possess or own these relationships and recognise the opportunity on a daily basis of seeing and focusing only on what is positive, the things that we like or love about that relationship, will eventually blossom.

However, it is important to say that this does not mean we live in denial and do not acknowledge relationships that do not enhance us through any behaviour that does not honour the relationship. These acts, which do not honour the relationship must be highlighted and addressed quickly so that both parties understand clearly what is acceptable and what is not acceptable. If the relationship is of equal importance to both parties, the necessary adjustments will be made immediately. If the adjustments are not made, you may have to re-evaluate the relationship.

Energy flows where your attention goes
Where's your energy flowing?

Chapter 7

Principle 5:
The Law of Persistence

If at first you don't succeed try, then try, try again.

There are two dates that are significant to every person's life — the day you were born and the day you realise why you were born.

Thomas Edison invented the light bulb on November 4th 1879 after many a failed attempt. When a reporter asked him about his many failures, which have been said to have exceeded over 1,000 attempts, Edison simply said, "It just meant that I was that many times closer to success".

But how does a person have the wherewithal to keep going in the face of failure? The word persistence in the dictionary is described as tenacity, determination, doggedness, resolve, diligence, resolution, abstinence, stubbornness, tirelessness, endurance, purpose, dedication, devotion and drive.

Looking at my students that have gone on to achieve success, I notice that they all have a particular mindset. Their mind is set on their end goal, which is depicted through an image of where they see themselves in the future. Through the process of applying the Y-factor, they are extremely clear as to why they must travel and reach the identified destination and once they have applied the Y-Factor that is all they see to the exclusion of almost everything else. So actually, the persistence that the onlooker sees is not really persistence to the person doing the work. To them they are just going after that thing they see in their mind and are trying to reach it and manifest it from mind to matter. They are operating with the "end goal in mind" and this appears to be an important key factor.

In any endeavour where one seeks a successful outcome, it is important that one begins with the end in mind — and this I mean quite literally. Whatever it is that you wish to experience, create it in as much detail as possible within your mind's eye and store it there. Remember we said that the mind is like an incubator.

A man cannot experience what he cannot conceive - the reverse is also true.

In addition to having an image of what your future looks like, give that image life by noticing not only what that future looks like, but also smells like, sounds like and feels like. Make it as real as you can in your mind's eye.

The law of persistence comes into its own only when there is a clear and detailed image in one's mind backed by a strong sense of "it is possible" coupled with—yes you guessed it— the Y-Factor why this objective must be achieved. It is usually linked with a deep-seated desire that is fuelled by an emotion such as anger at an injustice or a deep sense of compassion or love for others. Often it is anchored in a cause, goal, objective or purpose that has benefits for others, not just for self.

It is interesting to notice that professions such as architecture or medicine require up to seven years of study before one qualifies and is allowed to practice. Could this be linked to the fact that the professional bodies to which they belong need to be absolutely certain that they have attained the high standard required because if they have not attained this level of standard and practice at a poor standard it could result in the loss of life? Over this seven-year period as undergraduates, the student must be committed, dedicated and maintain a steady persistence throughout.

The great songwriter R Kelly has been known to lock himself in his room for days when he's composing a new work of art. He interacts and speaks with no one. It is said that even his meals have to be left on a tray by his door; that is the level of his devotion to his art and craft.

It is my belief that we are all born with a unique gift and when we identify and express this gift we are seen as a genius. This special unique gift comes in the form of a special "gene-in-us" that is geared towards success. That special "gene-in-us" knows what success in its unique form is for us. And when we honour this special "gene-in-us", it blesses us by others seeing this gene and marvelling at how it manifests through us. In amazement, all they can say is "PURE GENIUS" when they see its fruits.

However, unfortunately through other people's ideas, suggestions and directives, most of us lose touch with this success gene-in-us and as a result lose our way and lose our GPS.

The 10,000 Hour rule

Forty years ago, in a paper a paper called *American Scientist*, Herbert Simon and William Chase drew one of the most famous conclusions in the study of expertise showing that there are no instant experts in chess.

Their study determined that for a person to reach grandmaster level, this required no less than about a decade's intense preoccupation with the game. They stated that a master had spent perhaps 10,000 to 50,000 hours staring at chess positions.

In the years that followed, an entire field within psychology grew up devoted to elaborating on Simon and Chase's observation — and researchers, time and again, reached the same conclusion: it takes *a lot* of practice to be good at complex tasks.

After Simon and Chase's paper, for example, the psychologist John Hayes looked at seventy-six famous classical composers and found that in almost every case, those composers did not create their greatest work until they had been composing for at least ten years. (The sole exceptions: Shostakovich and Paganini, who took nine years, and Erik Satie, who took eight.)

In the bestselling book *Outliers,* the story of success by Malcolm Gladwell (a must read for the success connoisseur), he wrote about the "ten-thousand-hour rule." Simply put, this theory states that on average it takes about 10,000 hours of practice or about 10 years to achieve and operate at a very high standard.

He also states that no one succeeds at a high level without innate TALENT: "achievement is talent plus preparation." The ten-thousand-hour theory illustrates that "the closer psychologists look at the careers of the gifted, the smaller the role innate talent seems to play and the bigger the role preparation seems to play."

After working directly with young people for over 20 years, I am convinced that when parents fully understand this concept they will understand why they must invest so much in their children's early years—the payoff in the future will be incalculable. This is one of the aims of the GPS System—to introduce this idea of preparing your mind for success before it begins to set (around 17-22 years).

When parents engage in the process of identifying a child's gifts, talents and abilities in the earliest stages of the child's life, it establishes a foundation within the child at a very early stage which one can now build upon. This is then reinforced with the Y-Factor as to why a particular talent opposed to another must be practiced. If the Y-Factor contains within it the reasoning that the person enjoys the practice or is naturally good at it, the practice won't feel like hard work; in fact, it won't feel like work at all. This gives the child the competitive edge over another who is merely putting in the work. The one who has found the "special gene-in-us" never tires and just keeps on going because it really isn't work. It's more fun than work.

My daughter told me that she had her earliest memories of wanting to be a singer at age 8. I must confess that I did not take her seriously until she was around 14. I will never forget the event that brought this awareness to me. She came home and told me that she had been to the dentist and that they had removed 4 perfectly good teeth. Somehow she had convinced them that her teeth were overlapping, hence why she needed teeth removed. This was only the first stage. She then had to wear braces, which on occasion where excruciatingly painful, followed by a long period of wearing "retainers" as the process of pulling her teeth together was achieved. She shared with me that this was the end goal— she wanted to have a perfect smile because she was going to be a singer. Now you may say that was crazy, but for me I saw a young person who only saw her end goal and saw it so clearly that the pain was incidental. She was focused on the end goal.

By the time she was 18, people were always commenting on her vocal ability, not realising that she had already been persistently practicing hard for 10 years.

Acie is without exception one of the most outstanding students I have ever had the opportunity to teach.

From our first meeting at his interview, I noted that there was something different about this young man. He was a very confident young man who found himself as a young toddler transported here to London for his own safety from his native Zimbabwe due to troubles back home.

Acie had settled well in the UK and was a very bright young man. He had achieved very good grades at school, but had a passion for music. As a result, he had decided to take a year off to pursue his passion and see where it led him. That was how he was led to Urban Voice UK. He enrolled onto our 12 week music plus programme and was excited about the prospect of doing music.

Within 4 weeks, it became apparent to me that this man had much more to give. We struck a good relationship, but it was no different to the one I had with other students.

Then one day that all changed. It started off as a normal day. I had got up as normal, gone in to the office as normal, everything was fine. Then around 11:00 am, I noticed that Acie was missing. I was told that there had been a fire at Acie's home, which caused me great alarm. But what caused me more surprise was when I saw Acie appear after lunch. He said that he had dealt with the fire and didn't want the fire to stop him.

I was blown away by his attitude.

A few weeks after this incident, Acie approached me asking me if I would mentor him. I agreed and thereafter we met regularly over the next 9 months. During this time, I discovered what he was really passionate about. It wasn't music he was passionate about, but the rights of young people and the many injustices that they often suffered from. Acie had real life and brutal experience of this back home in Zimbabwe.

Once we both discovered this, over the next few months we put together his dream plan.

This passion for the rights of young people led him to join the Youth Parliament, where he soon rose amongst the ranks and eventually became the head of the Youth Parliament here in the UK, and delivered a fantastic speech to the House of Commons. He then applied to Harvard University, was invited to attend an interview and was accepted.

Today, he is back home in Zimbabwe, working as part of the Government there. His department? You guessed it — Youth.

Acie's execution of the blueprint we shaped during the mentorship actually shocked me.

That's when the importance of coaching and mentoring really hit me.

It then dawned on me that perhaps it was because I had found a mentor at such an early age that this had made a huge impact on my life. I began to appreciate my mentor so much more and he soon was to suggest to me that I consider taking up mentoring and coaching based on what I had learnt from him over so many years.

Now I have regular mentoring sessions with my mentor and place a much higher value and emphasis on these sessions. In fact, I have set an intention to have a mentor for every important area of my life. Why not? If it has worked in one area of my life, why not extend the principle to all important areas of one's life?

In the summer of 2012 as I watched the London Olympics, I got a mighty revelation about what it takes to become an Olympian.

From all over the world, the world's very best athletes flew in to London to compete for an Olympic medal. Then all of a sudden it hit me.

What one thing does every one of these athletes share in common? A coach — what a revelation. Then I remembered one of my son's training sessions many years ago. His coach had set him 4 x 400 metres laps with a 20 second rest between each lap and a crazy target time for each lap. Once this was completed, he was given a 5 minute rest and had to do it all again twice. It was the end of the second set of 4 x 400 metres and Joshua collapsed on the ground, saying he couldn't run another inch. I watched in total amazement what happened next. As the clock ticked, Josh was still stretched out on the ground. As the clock wound down to the last 30 seconds, Joshua's coach started yelling to Joshua to get up and get round that track. Joshua got up. The coach said, "Get set...GO!" Joshua started running. By the time he had completed the second lap, he was now running on something else — his mind; his will had taken over. I watched in amazement as I saw this guy who a few minutes ago was laid out on the ground, now running around the track 4 times. By the end of the 4th lap he collapsed in a heap on the ground, something that the other athletes were clearly familiar with as a few of his teammates surrounded him, some pouring water into his month whilst others massaged his legs. Then due to the amount of lactic acid in his system, he threw up. It was a sight and that was when my respect for athletes not only increased tenfold, but I experienced a crucial lesson about the need for a coach, which Josh would later confirm.

You see, when you find a coach who you connect with, trust and who understands you and knows what you want to achieve, his role and purpose is to push you beyond what you think you can't endure because the truth is you can endure much more than you think. Joshua clearly showed me that.

So I am now of the opinion that you cannot be your very best unless you have a coach to support and push you in that important area of your life. The coach can take many forms, but is essentially that person who can set you a goal or target that you just go for without thinking about it, trusting that they know your limits and your true potential and can guide you towards it.

Chapter 8

Principle 6:
The Law of High Quality Service

When what you truly are supports what you truly want, the
Universe says YES. — Bro Ishmael

The Secret law of giving

In ancient times before money was invented, people still were able to do business. How? Through the barter system. In those days, people simply exchanged what they had for what they wanted. For example, if I had a farm and had 100 chickens and you had a farm with 100 cows and 1 day I woke up and thought to myself *I fancy some beef stew today for my family,* the easiest and simplest way for me to get some beef would be to pay you a visit and barter with you, i.e., offer you some of my chickens in exchange for your cow. We would eventually settle on the numbers of chickens for the cow and then the exchange would take place. The deal would be done, the exchange would take place and with both parties satisfied each would go on his merry way. That was the barter system.

However, there was a problem with this method of doing business. If I wanted your cow but you did not want my chickens, because you had just completed a deal for chickens the previous day, how was I going to get my beef to make my beef stew?

This is a very simplistic scenario and I use it to illustrate why it was necessary to produce a medium that all parties could recognise as valuable and thus save people having to transport large items to be exchanged.

My mentor highlighted to me that this was the primary basis why money was created—as a "symbol" to represent that agreed, common medium. Money in and of itself is nothing other than printed-paper. It is the meaning we give to it through collective awareness that makes it valuable.

Money is merely the representation of 2 things –

1. What you have
2. What you release

Let us return to the farmer story. Once it became clear that offering chickens was not going to get me my cow to make my beef stew, I could turn around dejected and return home empty handed or I could think and then ask the other farmer a question that would create new possibilities through which I might still obtain my cow. The question being "What service could I render to you for which you would be willing to pay me a cow?" Once the farmer determined the service I could render him and I was in agreement, I could carry out the duty and the cow would be mine.

Money is merely a physical thing symbolising movement of an invisible thing.

The invisible thing is energy, which each and every one of us possesses. This can be given in the form of service rendered to another for which we are recompensed. It is the most valuable of all our possessions for through its release do we acquire and achieve everything else.

The slave trade depicts and illustrates this most clearly. The slave masters where not interested in the possessions of their slaves; it was the individual and the healthy body the slave possessed (the other most valuable possession we possess) through which this energy could be expressed.

Putting this theory to the test was one of my early great challenges and what I have since termed "My Great experiment" as I found myself setting out on the Urban Voice mission with no money or physical resources with which to start. However, equipped with just a vision and my energy which was fuelled by my passion, today more than 20 years later, I have invested over 1 million pounds through Urban Voice UK and other companies into supporting and empowering young people so they may live fulfilled lives. This has impacted well over 100,000 young people with some having attained household name status.

My mentor was right

Many people focus on what they want, often not asking why they think they have this need. Many also give very little thought, if any, to what they possess and therefore what they can give as quality service in exchange for the thing desired.

What you are is more valuable than anything else. I believe this is what one of my favourite Reggae artists Freddie McGregor was conveying through his song "To be poor is a crime" http://bit.ly/18sJKwI.

To be poor is a crime because it actually illustrates the fact that both Principle 5: The Law of Gratitude and Principle 6: The Law of High Quality Service are not present in one's life. Let me explain. To know that you can offer, give or provide some service for which you can receive some form of recompense is both liberating and empowering. These are both qualities that one should appreciate and be grateful for, as they illustrate that there is something you can do to liberate your present situation. Your role is simply to figure out "what is it that I can do?" "Signing on" to receive benefits therefore should be something one does only in the most desperate of circumstances and should be used as a means of last resort whilst one is planning a route out of this predicament.

One who is poor is one who has not woken up to the fact that there is something they can do, and if Farrah Gray, the son of a poor black family, can become a millionaire during his early teens whilst still at school, there is something you can do. If, more recently, a young kid nicknamed "Tiny Trump", the son of a single Canadian mum can become a millionaire at 7 – Yes 7! – there is something you can do! Please Google these names and read about them so that you can become inspired.

Givers and Takers

I have come to realise in life that there are two kinds of people, givers and takers, and we would do well to work out which one we are. Steven Covey, in his book *The 7 Habits of Highly Effective People* (another book I highly recommend), wrote about a different way of doing business. He talked about the win-win model which is actually derived from the barter system, i.e., both parties must benefit equally.

Unfortunately, this approach is not yet a popular one. Many feel that taking or getting is the name of the game and this can be seen through individual relationships 1 on 1, as well as with business to business. It's all about winner takes all. However, I believe the game has just changed and the name of the new game is about how much you can give through high quality service and those who are still playing the old game are finding things increasingly tougher.

It is interesting to note that in the Jewish community, who are considered one of the wealthiest people on the planet, their measure of one who is successful is not measured by how much one has, but by how much one gives. Think about that for a moment.

Focusing on being a giver changes your mindset at a deep subconscious level. Firstly, it empowers you because it wakes you up to the realisation and appreciation of what you have, as you cannot give what you do not have. You got to have surplus if you can donate 1 million pounds to a charity. Secondly, it makes you become conscious on how you give, as you are aware that the purpose behind your giving is to support someone or something else. Let me illustrate. If you see a beggar on the street corner daily begging for money, is providing him with a big donation every day supporting him or making him dependent on you?

My mentor challenged me once saying to me, "Try to out-give life". This was based on one of his philosophies which follows:

No deed goes unrewarded

The reward may not come through the expected channel, but come it will as I have found through experimenting and putting this theory to the test many times. It is now an enshrined part of my life and I even have a term for it. I call it *"The secret law of giving"*.

Nelson Mandela epitomizes The Secret Law of giving

As I write this book, the passing of Nelson Mandela has just been announced. May he rest in peace. What a great example and display of this principle of high quality service in action. Nelson Mandela gave 27 years of his life for a cause greater than himself, he gave 27 years for what he believed in, standing against his oppressors. In the end, his reward did not come through his oppressors, but through the rest of the world as he was acknowledged as the greatest statesman the world has known in over a century. This is the power of high quality service and the secret law of giving.

And so it is that I ask you, as you ponder this principle in relation to your own life, what are you willing to give for a cause greater than yourself? Reflecting upon and answering this question will open you up to amazing new experiences, if you are diligent and sincere. Don't take my word for it; test it for yourself.

The proof is always in the practice

In a recent interview, Richard Branson stated that he thought the future for mankind was through enough people finding a niche problem that they passionately cared about wanting to solve, then starting a business that offered a solution to that niche problem. Does that remind you of our young entrepreneurs at the beginning of this book? Branson also started his life as an entrepreneur with hardly any money, but devoted all his time and energy not to making money, but to trying to fix a problem he cared passionately about. He dropped out of school and started a magazine that was dealing with issues he felt strongly and passionately about, like the Vietnam War.

Finding your passion leads you to your purpose and then to fulfilment.

Like Richard Branson, at the beginning of my journey I also had a passion that I cared passionately about. I cared passionately about the right for my young children to be able to see and have a relationship with me, their father. I was also passionate about music and providing platforms for young people through which they and I (as a young person back then) could express and develop our creativity. Soon I discovered that I could combine these two passions and the mix would reveal to me my purpose and give me the tools to define what it is that I do. It's great to get a good job and

117

start a career, but in my opinion it's far more rewarding to find your purpose, pursuing your passion and making a difference in the world.

I believe making a difference in the world is the new personal driver for us all. About two years ago I conducted a study where I interviewed approximately 1,000 individuals who were from the banking and financial sectors (from the top 5% earners bracket) about their job, career, industry and personal life. I was amazed at the results.

- Approximately 25% were unhappy with their job using words like soulless, just playing with numbers
- Approximately 12.5% were planning an exit strategy to do something more meaningful and fulfilling
- Approximately 15% felt trapped, i.e., did not like their current job at all but did not know what else they could do
- Staggeringly more than 70% expressed that they were either not happy or fulfilled and that ideally they would like to be doing something more fulfilling that made more of a direct impact in society

Another part of this research was to test the theory of focusing on the intent of wanting to give quality service. The experiment consisted of me engaging with total strangers for no more that 5 minutes in which time I told them about Urban Voice, the work of the organisation and a project that we wanted to deliver but required additional funds. The results were amazing:

In more than 50% of cases, these total strangers took out cash and gave it to me, a total stranger as a contribution to the project. I concluded the experiment when a complete stranger, a modest man so I shall not reveal his name, invited me to his office a couple weeks after our 3-minute first conversation when we met whilst standing outside the

Mayfair Hotel. After telling him about the organisation and one project with young disadvantaged youth, he gave me his card and said to give him a call, which I did the following week. He then invited me to his office for a cup of tea.

His office only turned out to be the Headquarters of Lend Lease. In case you don't know who Lend Lease are, they are the company partially responsible for building the Olympic Village. The result of that afternoon tea at his office was Lend Lease Governors club (the charity division) handing over a cheque to Urban Voice UK of 4 figures, plus providing support in the way of staff, food, drink and the plushest board rooms for the filming of our Youth Get Real dinner discussion which was also partly funded by the Home Office and was a response to the riots that rocked the country back in 2011. As a result of this support, we were able to pay a film crew to film, and edit the sessions and, you can now watch the Youth Get Real dinner discussions by following the link http://bit.ly/1cZMyCY or by going directly to the Urban Voice UK website http://www.urbanvoiceuk.com.

Turning your Passion-In2-Profits

Richard Branson was able to turn his Passion-In2-Profits and I am convinced that identifying what you're passionate about and figuring out how you can align providing goods and services with your passion or passions is the fastest way to get out of the "Rat Race" — you'll never spend another day working slavishly; you'll find yourself simply doing what you love. Life takes on a whole new meaning and you find that you have more life, energy and vitality with which you engage in your passion. It does not feel like work and so you find that you are not clock watching; rather, time seems to speed up, i.e., you look up from your activity and in what seemed like 30 mins and you realise a whole hour has gone.

The concept of turning Passion-In2-Profits is a hard concept for many to grasp. I know this as I have preached this for the last 20 years.

During early 2013, I took a weekend course with a company called The Internet Business School. This course introduced me to the world of Internet Marketing. The founder of The Internet Business School was a multi-millionaire who perfectly illustrated and proved this theory of one being able to turn their Passion-In2-Profits, beyond any doubt.

The story of how Simon Coulson came to become a millionaire is a funny and intriguing one. He took redundancy from his job at BT to pursue his passion as a musician and singer. Whilst doing his music, he invested most of his redundancy into a van for the band and the remainder into property in Europe just because it sounded like a good idea and the funds were big enough to buy a property anywhere else. He then came across internet marketing and decided to put together an information product, which he advertised online. He soon found that he was making more money online than he was making from his music gigs, providing high quality service through his information products. How are we assured that they were high quality products? Lots of people were willing and did pay for them. Before he knew it, he had a thriving Internet Business.

The point to note here is that pursuing his passion freed him from his 9-5 and provided him with the time and space to think creatively about what he wanted to do.

In turning your Passion-In2-Profits, you need creativity and the worlds of business and work, which hitherto did not give much respect to creative individuals, are finally waking up to the fact that we all have and need to employ our creativity.

If you have a creative around you, pay them well or someone else will. Simon still regularly performs with his band at any given opportunity; however, he has since made over 10 million pounds through doing business on the Internet. Go to www.growpersonalsuccess.com where you will be able to receive a FREE gift (Online introductory video on making money on the Internet).

A Car Cleaning Business with a difference

An individual's passion can be a rare and obscure thing. Take Barry, for example, who I have had the good fortune of knowing for most of his life and mentored for a few years. Barry owns and runs a Bespoke Automotive Mobile car valeting business called B-Kleen for cars in London and the surrounding areas. He started his business in the summer of 2006 at the age of 21, soon after he finished and obtained his business degree. Having graduated, Barry looked at different career paths before finally deciding that self-employment was the most attractive for him. The question was self-employment doing what? Barry had always had a passion for cars and anything automotive, so a vehicle-related business was inevitable.

As a young boy, cleaning the car with his Dad was always an exciting and enjoyable time for him, which he always looked forward to. So one day he decided he was going to turn this passion into a business. I remember the first time he told me that he was starting a car cleaning business. I had to do a double take as I looked at him saying, "Are you sure about this?" By the time he had finished talking to me telling me why, I felt his passion for cars and realised he didn't want to do this—he needed to do this; that's how much the idea had caught a hold of him.

With very little finance, Barry began researching into how to piece together his own mobile unit. Armed with a £1,000 loan from his dad, he produced some business cards, purchased a second-hand vacuum and an old rusty Transit van. B-Kleen was born and Barry was up and running.

Barry's business has grown steadily over the years from strength to strength and his client list now includes: John Lewis, Toyota, Lexus, Bernard Marcus, Bushells, Rob van Helden and a host of other high profile clients, including none other than Abramovich, the owner of Arsenal football club. But it was not always like this. Let me give you another example of the power of high quality service. When Barry first started out, he did not know how to price his jobs and did price his jobs too cheap, but he always gave high quality service. Do you know how Barry found out that he was charging too little? Believe it or not, some of his customers began telling him, "The time that you spend cleaning our car and the quality service you give is too much for what you charge. You need to charge us more." After Barry heard that from 3 customers, he got the message. (If 3 or more people that do not know each other say the same thing to you, you need to take note whether you like what's been said or not—I live by this.) Barry increased his prices by over 30% and guess what happened? The problem customers disappeared and at the same time the high-end market was born. I know it sounds crazy and I wouldn't have believed it too, but I was there.

In early 2013, Barry began planning his expansion programme and now has begun secure contracts with Building Management companies beginning with FW Gapp Building Management company where he has the on-site valeting rights for the residents of Kensington Heights.

A classic story of someone with no experience who was able to identify his passion and then get creative, exploring how he could turn his passion into profits.

What is interesting about Barry is how his passion translates. Within the first few months of setting up the business, Barry had secured a number of clients simply due to one thing only—high quality service. Barry's meticulous attention to detail often saw his clients telling him to stop cleaning because they were happy with the service and had to go off to a meeting. Within 18 months, he found himself in the strangest position where some of his clients were telling him that he was charging too little for his service and that he needed to increase his prices. Now how many companies can boast of such a statement?

That is the power of high quality service; it literally draws money to you. Unfortunately, you may never have been taught this principle in school or college. Instead, you might have been told to focus on getting that money. Well now you know that's back to front; always focus your energy on giving the highest quality service, not for the customer but for you first just because that's your standard and watch what happens. Yet again, put it to the test. Readers of The GPS System can receive a special discount on his car cleaning service when you register at http://www.growpersonalsuccess.com.

Time flies when you're having fun

After more than 20 years of what I can only refer to as being blessed to be in the position where I have been able to pursue my passion, find my purpose and gain fulfilment from what I do, I am convinced that such a journey brings a number of benefits for the traveller.

These benefits are:

- Psychological, in terms of a more balanced and peaceful mind which suffers from less stress than most
- Physiological, in terms of being more youthful in both your appearance and energy levels as a result of being able to engage in a lifestyle which is full of health and vitality
- An increased sense of well-being, in terms of generally a more optimistic outlook on life
- Richer, deeper more authentic human connections through meaningful relationships

Chapter 9

Principle 7:
The Law of Honouring Thyself

Don't set goals; set values. What is your value system? Create it and then live by it.

From these values that you have identified (and I encourage that you write down as many as you can and refer to them regularly), you can then create goals that are based on these, your values. This provides a solid foundation for your life, creating your personal integrity. To illustrate this, we all recognise that money is a necessary commodity that we all need to assist us through life. However, in pursuit of it, would you become a drug dealer? Whether your answer is yes or no (though I hope it's no), it is based on your personal value system. So defining clearly your value system and honouring yourself through living by this value system creates what I can only describe as an invisible but tangible energy around you that although invisible to the naked eye is picked up by any and everyone who engages with you. Often times people will not be able to put their finger on it, but they will notice it, saying things like, "he's got a good vibe," or "there is something about her that I just can't put my finger on," or "you've got good energy." I call it being congruent and by this I mean when your deepest intent, your thoughts, your words and your actions are all in alignment.

This is one of the most difficult of the principles to adopt because it forces us to look at ourselves and often times we don't want to do this because we know we may not like aspects of what we see. Even worse, is that if we then don't take action to remedy this, then we effectively are walking around in denial, adding to our discomfort.

Here is a story of one young man whose mentorship with me was brief but profound and illustrates how this principle when practiced can work with such amazing effect that I thought I'd let him tell the story in his own words.

*When I was 17 years old, I lied my way through an application to be accepted on to a Grad-scheme internship at Bloomberg LP. I faced a dual interview with two people, who asked me a tonne of questions that I was unfamiliar with (my first ever corporate interview). At the end of the conversation, we ended up sharing stories about things that we had in common, and in fact they took to me very well. One thing that they mentioned was that I kept it real, up until the point whereby they asked me how university was going – **yikes**. I then had to confess that I was not a university student; I hadn't even received my A-level results. At this point I was trembling. There was nothing more that I wanted than this internship. Fortunately, I received a call a few weeks later and was told the good news (on my birthday) that I was accepted onto the programme.* (Role: Sales and Analytics)

When I joined the company, I was placed on the Sales team which covered the Netherlands. I settled in with a nice team. Everybody was focused and friendly; however, there was a young man in particular whom I got on with really well. His name was Nasir.

I was never fond of university, and I didn't think that this was a path that I wanted to take to succeed. Now back to the internship... Nasir and I got along very well and we shared similar views too. He did not attend university and he joined the company fresh out of college as an intern and moved up to managing accounts by the age of 24. Having only spent 3 weeks with him, Nasir was offered an opportunity at a Brokerage as a VP, to which he up and left.

I had continued with my internship, keeping him in mind as a source of motivation. Unfortunately, I did not get offered a job at the end of my internship. The reason given seemed very vague, and an ex-colleague told me later that managers were concerned of my age. Regardless, the feedback was good and I was offered another internship for the following year.

Fast-forward 2 years – I decided to give university a chance, test my doubts and see where I got with it. I held on to it for a whole year; however, I still knew that it was not for me. By the latter half of my academic year, I was already trying to find myself back into the city.

I read in the newspaper that there was a city wiz trader who made a tonne of money. I looked at the dude like "psshh, I can do it too". I researched the company that he worked for and sent an email every 3 days requesting an opportunity. My proposal did not mention any salary or any risk, just simply the opportunity to learn. My hunger was pure and it was not blinded with vanity; I was eager to learn.

By the 6th week, the managing director sent me an email admiring my determination and consistency and way with words. And for those reasons, I was offered an internship as a trainee at their small propriety-trading firm. I spent 7 months at this firm and learnt so much. I shifted from learning about Government Bonds to Commodity contracts. On my time learning about commodities, I was in need of help from an old friend at Bloomberg who specialised in this area.

After meeting up for lunch with her, she told me that she was the partner of Nasir! The guy whom I had met 3 years ago. Anyway, it was great meeting up with her, and she too shared the same thought. She spoke about me to Nasir, and surprisingly he remembered everything about me, making reference to my unique character. A few days later, I received a call from Nasir. I was shocked as to why he wanted to reach out to me. After catching up for 5-7 minutes max, he wanted to meet me for lunch, and within the same conversation offered me a job as an Equity Sales Trader – permitting that I spoke Italian, which I didn't (lol). So I didn't get the job. Regardless, I received a phone call from Nasir, talking to me about putting me in touch with the Trading desk, and how they were searching for the right fit to join the Asia desk as a Junior Equity Trader.

It wasn't until a few months later that things began to become concrete, and in the interim I did nothing but toss and turn in my sleep! I received an email at 11pm from the Head of the Asia Desk, who told me that he heard nothing but good things about me... and he wanted to " have a chat " that morning .... 5am in the morning! Lucky I hadn't slept yet, so I was fortunate to catch the email! I got up 4 hours later and gave a good impression. Truth is, I didn't get much sleep; I was up for hours planning questions and potential answers. However, I was so frustrated because I began to drift away from being myself and keeping it real.

I was running late and I ended up taking a black cab to the city in the hope that it would pay off! I forgot to mention that he wanted to have a chat with me in Starbucks. Now picture this... 5am, in the city, in December with not a person in sight...without a clue as to who you are meeting. Like my first ever interview, the man came down with his colleague. We orders coffees and the phrase "having a chat" was erased! I was given a full on interview in an environment that I was not used to, with interviewers I did not prepare for!

With no preparation, no plan...all I had left was my words and my balls.

I kept it real and told them the truth, told them my age, my vision and what I had to bring to the table (hunger, drive, youth, eagerness, humility). I spoke with confidence, but deep down I was shaking. Regardless, that was it; I was put on the spot with aggressive market players and I had no choice but to prove that they made the right decision. After 30 minutes of conversation, the two men who interviewed me left the Starbucks with no handshake or smile, simply a "we'll be in touch" – which meant absolutely nothing at the time.

Almost 6 weeks went by and I did not hear from them. I met up with Tony Biola — the dad of one of my closest friends, who has inspired me in many ways — to catch up. Not knowing what I went through over the recent months, I broke down the details on what had been happening in my world. I explained to him that I was restless and anxious about this opportunity, to the point whereby I became pessimistic towards its potential. Throughout the whole conversation, he could see the fear and doubt in my eyes. Towards the end of my vent, he spoke to me about my generation, and how there was a change in the atmosphere...an indescribable vibration across the youth that was absent with his generation...the only word that could describe this was Energy. With energy, he wasn't describing electric waves as such, but the uniqueness that expresses through our touch, our aura and appearance when we keep it real with ourselves, with a clear sense of knowing how we want to show up in the world. This energy that comes from that deep authentic place within each and every person. This energy, he shared, was developed from "honouring you", but before this one must come to understand oneself through self-discovery, through defining a purpose for your life and engaging with others through and from this authentic place. He told me that I had nothing to worry about, although how I described the interview was terrible. He picked up on the responses that the interviewers made, coupled with the answers that I gave and told me that I had not a thing to worry about.

Soon after this meeting with Uncle T, I was invited into their office for an induction, and moreover to be exposed to the field that I would potentially get into. During my talks with Uncle T, he spoke to me about the laws of energy, and how letting this precious commodity shine would be the key to my successes. I didn't quite understand the true meaning behind this, especially if they have a certain calibre of academia that they would like to maintain in the corporate world; how would creating energy alone open doors for you?

It was the 1ˢᵗ of January when I had my induction day. I stepped into the office nervous; however, I kept in mind the conversation that I had with Uncle T. I had studied as much as possible about the business and the industry. However, reverting back to the importance of creating energy, I decided to put the information that I crammed to one side and build rapport with the traders on the desk. It was amazing to see how the conversation started off from talking about graphs and technical analysis, to our favourite TV shows and holidays. It wasn't about the topics that created energy; however, within such topics came ideas and viewpoints, which in turn reflect one's character. Before I knew it, the head of the desk pulled me to one side and told me that I have something unique. To my amazement, he then said, "We like your energy" and that not only did he think that I would benefit from this opportunity, they too would gain something from bringing me on board. Regardless of whether I had a Master's degree (let alone bachelor's), and having front office experience, and most importantly my age... I would be the right fit for the business.

Within three weeks, I received the official phone call from the company, and within a week I was a fully licensed official Equity Trader!

What Xavier did not share was that with this appointment he became one of the youngest equity traders in the country. The average was around twenty-five; he was just twenty when he started.

Xavier is obviously an outstandingly talented young man. However, if he had not kept it real, been authentic and honoured himself by being congruent with his thoughts, words and actions would he have gotten the job? I am pretty certain he would not. Having spent a few years very close to city bankers, traders and some of the top 5% earners, I learnt that these guys are incredibly sharp and also many are very intuitive. They pick up on what's not said, your vibe, your posture, all kinds of things and they're usually looking for one thing, one thing that shows that you're not congruent and then you're out. Xavier did not give them that one thing; rather, he focused on keeping it so authentic. Just that word in his air to give him the confidence to be proud and say it like it was paid off and it was great to hear him screaming down the phone saying, "Uncle T I got the job and guess what? They said they liked my energy!"

The Truth behind the fall of JLS

This last story provides an interesting contrast.

The year was 2008 and it was the most difficult year in the history of Urban Voice UK. I had returned back to the organisation from my spell at the college and soon found myself at the front of delivering a £500,000 contract with little training as my right-hand colleague left at short notice. I was also responsible for delivering our Project Talent UK national urban talent project, which we had just launched from the Mayor's Office with additional support coming from Channel 4, MySpace, the Arts Council and Yamaha. I was under pressure, to say the least.

We had finished the national auditions and workshops and the final artist were selected and invited to join the other finalist in the Academy Training Boot camp to be staged in London. However at this stage all finalists were issued with contracts for signing, as we were incurring additional costs to the project born by my commercial company.

The artists were under no obligation. Some choose not to sign and that was fine. However, having demonstrated a track record over 15 years of having the ability to attract and work with outstanding urban talent before they hit success, such as Leona Lewis, Alexandra Burke, Richard Blackwood and Tinnie Tempah, I had a haunch that some of the acts I had selected had star potential and I had a plan to create a model, which was sustainable so that we could support new aspiring artists each and every year.

The day had arrived and I drove over to the venue to meet the artists who had made their way down from all parts of the country to attend the induction day.

The 20 artists all arrived, all signed contracts were collected and the artists settled in.

For the next seven days, they were totally under our care and responsibility. Breakfast lunch, dinner, travel fares, sleeping accommodation, the whole works—it was on me and my team and that was not including the intense fast track schedule they were to be subjected to, which was to simulate what a serious artist should know, and preparing them for the performance of their lives at the indigO$_2$.

Over the next seven days, the acts went through an intense programme, included training sessions starting at 6:00 am. Performance & vocal performance were followed by song-writing classes, studio recording sessions, photo shoots, radio interview training as well as live interviews on BBC Radio 1 Xtra and live performances.

It was a whirlwind of activity and my team was absolutely incredible. As the day drew nearer for their major performance at the O$_2$, it was electric. The night of the show, we had a debrief and all held hands and prayed as one team for a fantastic show.

I had invited most of the major record labels so everyone was poised to give their best performance.

It was a fantastic night and the audience loved every performance and artist. It was an event to be proud of. We were the first voluntary sector organisation to stage a concert at the indigO$_2$ in Greenwich. I, along with the judges, announced the winners. It was a close call between a group called Nutty NRG and a group called UFO. Nutty NRG narrowly beat UFO.

It was December 2007, and I was now having various discussion with some of the record labels who were present as well as beginning to explore how I might produce an album worth of recordings to showcase all the finalists. The project had overrun by 3 months mainly because of problems encountered by one of the project partners from the Mayor's office who let's say was far from the business of honouring herself. Meanwhile, I still had the students on the Music+ programme, plus the funders to deal with. I decided to take a much deserved break and flew off with my son to celebrate his birthday in Malaga.

On returning to the office in January, I was contacted by one of the members of UFO by email, then by phone requesting a meeting with me. They wanted to discuss the possibility of me managing them as artists. We set a meeting date. The meeting never took place and I never heard from him again. It soon became obvious why.

You see, UFO consisted of 4 guys called Marvin, Aston, Ortise and Jonathan you may probably know as the members of the group JLS. What I was soon to discover was that the reason why they did not attend the meeting was because they decided to enter X-Factor, even though they had a signed contract with me and even though the rules of X-Factor at the time clearly stated that you could not enter the competition if you had an existing contract with another company.

I made attempts to contact the boys to make them aware that I had been notified of their contractual breach; however, they made no attempt to respond.

I decided to watch how things would unfold.

After several weeks of preliminaries, the boys got through to the next stage of the X-Factor and then I started receiving calls to my office. I did not take the calls as I figured it was lawyers on behalf of either JLS or X-Factor and I wanted everything to be in writing. After several days, I then received a call on my phone from a private caller. It was their lawyers.

The lawyer told me that it had been brought to her attention that JLS had entered into X-Factor even though they were under contract to my commercial company. They asked me if I would FREE JLS from the contract. I invited them to put an offer to me in writing as I could see the boys had every chance of winning the competition. The following day I received a letter from the lawyers asking me to sign a deed of termination releasing the boys from their agreement. There was no mention of any financial remuneration I could not sign and till this day never did sign the document. I contacted my lawyers and after a fair exchange between both the lawyers I was advised that I would need substantial funds if I was to fight this case. I did not have access to the kinds of figures that were being suggested—£150k upwards. We made several attempts to contact the boys but by now they were shielded by the full muscle of the X-Factor. The fact that I was contacted by the boys' lawyers and the request was made proved that there was a valid contract in place and this was secretly known by the members of JLS and the legal team connected with them and the X-Factor.

The failure by the boys and their lawyers to handle this matter fairly and honourably meant that thousands of young people all over the country were denied the opportunity of chasing their dreams of a music career. Why? Because 50% of any remuneration received would have been utilised by

Urban Voice to produce an album showcasing the finalist, as we had done previously, as well as stage the competition — the following with further support from the Arts Council as the success of JLS would have demonstrated the need and benefit to young aspiring artist across the UK.

Then came the finals of X-Factor 2008 and I watched in amazement as I saw both 1st and 2nd place taken by ex-Urban Voice competition participants. However, I was particularly aggrieved, as this had been my plan, a chance to shine the spotlight on Urban Voice's ability to unearth and develop Urban Talent. My intention was to create a self-sustainable model that would ensure each year we were able to run this amazing project which resulted in at least three other finalists getting signed.

Without my knowledge, some of my team contacted some of the national tabloids and I soon found myself in a serious predicament. I was being offered large sums of money for the exclusive rights to the story. The predicament for me was this action would go against almost 20 years of work in supporting young people and now I was considering taking money to shop a story to the press about a group of young people. Somehow, I did not feel I was honouring myself or my work. In the end, I did not pursue it, much to the irritation of some of those in my team. I hoped that when things settled, the boys would meet with me and we would come to an amicable agreement. This never happened. Instead, their entire history was rewritten so as to wipe out any connection with Urban Voice. At a certain point, they released a movie in the cinema about the making of JLS which I went along to see if they would honour their humble beginnings with Urban Voice. Not a chance. But as I watched and listened, a realization dawned on me, which was that when you do not conduct yourself in a way that honours you, things may appear to look good, but ultimately you will not experience a sense of accomplishment or fulfilment long term. As I left the cinema annoyed at the partial truth I had just watched, I thought of the 6 hours of footage that we had locked away which showed JLS going through almost every form of assimilation needed to prepare for the X-Factor. I thought of releasing this to reveal the hidden story behind their success. But in the end, I decided against it.

We never did speak again until several years later when I bumped into one of them in a VIP booth at a Beyonce concert at the O_2. He had that look of shame and embarrassment as he greeted me saying that he would schedule a meeting between us. It never happened. A few weeks later, it was announced that the group was splitting up.

As rumour had it, they had been unsuccessful in breaking into America and now One Direction had come on the scene and had blown them out the teen pop market. There was nowhere else to go.

The irony in all of this was during the last weeks of the X-Factor finals back in 2008, unbeknown to the members of JLS, my team and I had a meeting with a representative from Puffy's label. They wanted to sign JLS. Just 1 year of success in the US is equivalent to 6 years of work in the UK, which is exactly the length of time the JLS project ran before they were dropped by their label.

Honour yourself is so important because it incorporates so many of the other principles. Let me illustrate. When you do not honour yourself, you dis-honour yourself. The word "dis" in the dictionary means to insult, disrespect, belittle, lessen and put down. Now we know the law of principle seven is to honour thyself; to dis-honour oneself is to literally go against oneself, to "cause" or initiate those things to belittle or lessen what you are. Once you do that, you immediately create (cause) a bypass, literally passing by the opportunity to activate Principle 2: The Power of Love. And remember, "the absence of Love is stagnation and decay".

So by dis-honouring you, YOU "cause" and take a bypass on the road that leads to love, ending up where stagnation and decay live.

This amounts to introducing Principle 3: The Law of the Mind, with scarcity as your focus, for decay is born out of anything that is reducing. This is the opposite of abundance.

Decay and a sense of reducing now as your focus leads to the misuse of Principle 4: The Law of Gratitude—what you focus on grows. JLS misused this principle to express gratitude where Urban Voice was concerned for whatever reason. Now let's be clear; no one is under any obligation to show gratitude to another. However, when you do not show gratitude or make it your focus not to show gratitude whenever and wherever possible, you are effectively working the law in reverse. The opposite of growth is....?

The reverse working of this principle and others now becomes your state of operation as you engage with Principle 5: The Law of Persistence, so you PERSIST in this negative operative state.

As a result, it is impossible to give sustained high quality service—Principle 6—because you are now effectively employing these universal principles in reverse.

To dis-honour yourself also goes against our defined definition of success and so will always ultimately lead you to a dead end.

Be congruent in your words, deeds and actions. By that I mean strive to synchronise your thoughts with your deeds and with your actions, not because you want to be a saint, but because you want to experience SUCCESS. This is the art of Growing Personal Success. Study this and it will pay you great dividends over time and if you should falter along the way, honour and embrace the learning, then move on and start over. Having learnt a new lesson, be stronger, wiser and better than before.

If only JLS had read this book.

Chapter 10

Conclusion: You Can Do It

To Thine own self be true. – Shakespeare

I hope you have enjoyed reading this book and the many stories I have shared. Through these stories, I hope you have come to see that you too can identify and Grow Your own Personal Success.

Success for you is POSSIBLE.

These are only a handful of the very many stories I could have shared that I have gathered over the last 20 years and through working with young people at Urban Voice UK, my not-for-profit organisation that empowers young people to live fulfilled lives. As I write these words, my organisation, which I consider my baby, is about to celebrate its 10th Anniversary.

I could have shared stories of many of my students, who as ex convicts for crimes such as drug dealing, gang violence and even murder, have come out of the prison system with no clear sense of direction.

Finding and enrolling on to our music and creative programmes at Urban Voice UK, they have been able to find their voice through revaluating their life, identifying their passion and purpose, as well as re-defining what success means to them. Often gaining clarity on these things for the first time in many cases was a major milestone from which most were able to then grow their personal vision of success, having found their voice. Once having found their voice, I have noticed that without exception over time they became transformed. Having found their voice, they become preoccupied with wanting to inspire others to find their voice.

They inspire others through setting and achieving new goals based on their new set of values and sharing these experiences with others. This can be illustrated through the examples such as retuning to college to gain qualifications, going to University and obtaining a degree, creating their own economy as an entrepreneur and even setting up in business. In a couple of instances, having set up a new business, they have even gone on to surpass their own expectations through being recognised and nominated for awards by the London Mayor's office.

These tried and tested universal principles work if applied diligently.

The famous writer Stephen Covey, in his bestselling book *The 7 Habits of Highly Effective People*, writes about just that — the habits of highly effective and therefore successful people. (I strongly recommend reading this book). The book was 1st published in 1989, two years before I began my practical journey to test the theories I had learnt from my mentor over the previous 10 years. I often refer to this journey as "My Great Experiment", as it was the process by which I was able to test the new theories I had been introduced to. *7 Habits of Highly Effective People* has been read by over 25 million people globally since it was first published more than 25 years ago, becoming an international phenomena of the literary world. It has been read by all kinds of people, including world leaders, business owners, scholars, parents and all types of people who seek to be more effective in organisations, businesses and in their personal lives.

This book was followed in 2004 by *The 8th Habit: From Effectiveness to Greatness*. Stephen writes in *The 8th Habit* that due to the rapidly changing world and the new demands placed on all of us, greatness must now build upon effectiveness if people are to excel and thrive in this new technological and information age. In this new age, money is not the thing that those who thrive and excel seek; it is fulfilment through passionate execution and significant contribution. Stephen goes on to write that *"greatness comes through finding your voice and helping others to find theirs."*

This, he writes, is the crucial challenge in the world today and this is the 8th Habit.

He describes your "Voice" as containing 3 elements.

1) Your passion—what you love doing.
2) Your talent—what you are naturally good at (everyone is good at something; you just might not know what it is yet).
3) Demand—what the world needs and will pay you for.

As I sit writing this final chapter, I am struck by the effects of the Principle 5: The Law of Gratitude. When you give from a place of gratitude, you always receive from a source or sources that you least expect. And so it that as I sit here writing this final chapter, one of my brightest students, who I sponsored on to the GPS Programme as a gift in appreciation for his service and support of the vision, drew my attention to the similarities between Stephen Covey and myself through our respective journeys during the 90's. He also drew my attention to the uncanny similar philosophy behind Urban Voice UK and *The 8th Habit*. On closer examination we noticed that both were introduced to the world within one year of each other—Urban Voice UK was established 1 year before *The 8th Habit* was published in 2004. The only difference being one illustrated this philosophy theoretically, the other practically. The gift I received and now share with you was the absolute clarity that this is not just a labour of love; "It's my thing", it is my purpose. Through finding my voice, I live for helping others find theirs and that includes you.

Urban Voice UK represents that platform which was established for young people who equally have a voice and have something that they too wish to share, contribute or do.

For the first time in history, young people have a chance to impact the world in ways that simply were never possible before. Consider the young black American, Farrah Gray, who displayed his entrepreneurial streak at the age of around seven when he started selling rocks with his unique stamp to local residents. By the time he was thirteen, he was a millionaire.

Or consider the young Canadian Tiny Trump who was a millionaire at the age of 7. He started in business at the age of 3.

Closer to home here in the UK, I have met young teenagers who are generating 5 figures a month in their business. Don't just take my word for it; check these names out for yourself, do your research. For doing this will help prove and firmly establish within the area of your logical mind (left brain) that success for you is possible. If they can do it, so can you. You just have to get clarity right away through finding your voice.

So how does one find their voice and how do we help you find yours?

This book introduces you to the new way of looking at YOU so as to discover your voice. The GPS 1-day workshop, 3-day weekend course and 10-week mentoring programme guides you on your journey along this new path of self-discovery and personal development.

On any great voyage you need a navigation system. Grow Personal Success is the navigation system for finding your voice. Once you've found your voice, you'll have found health, wealth and happiness in abundance.

I hope this book has helped transform the way you see yourself through revaluating what is really important to you, what you are really passionate about, and defining a new vision of success and what it looks like, feels like, sounds and smells like. Taste your success!

Once discovered, I hope you will pursue your newfound purpose with passion, so that you can ultimately experience fulfilment and a new life that will amaze you.

You have the chance to do something amazing with your life. Why not take a hold of that chance and do something NOW? Plant the seed today, begin today not tomorrow, for as my mentor once told me "Today, right NOW is all that we really have".

The past has gone and the future has not arrived yet. This is why the PRESENT is named as such; it is the most precious of all gifts that life has given to us. With this gift, you determine and create your future by the thoughts, feeling, beliefs, words and actions you chose. Use your present by setting as clear an intention as possible through definite clarity of purpose.

So right now, I challenge you over the next 7 days to implement as many of the principles into your life as often as you can and pay attention to notice what happens in and around you. Be on the constant lookout to apply any one of the principles.

I am confident that if diligently applied, you will make new discoveries within 7 days, making it difficult for you to not continue on your journey to Growing Personal Success. Go on what are you waiting for......

Remember you don't know what you don't know until someone shows you.

Once shown you must now choose to act.

Act, either like you don't know or Act like you do know, but act you must.

You must now make your choice ....

Remember, the magic is in the practice which is choosing daily to act, knowing that practice makes perfect.

Chapter 11

The Voyage Continues

Today, my "Great Experiment" continues with even more enthusiasm as I now know for certain that personal success is available to all if we are willing to go on the voyage of self discovery

As I pause to look back on the path travelled thus far, I see there has been much personal growth. I now look back at my childhood with all those challenges and am truly grateful for all of them, for I am able to find the positive seed in each seemingly negative experience and how that helped me determine what I did want and what I did not want as part of my life.

In order that you may grow your personal success, you must do the same. Remember it is not what happens to you that is important but how you choose to respond to what happens to you.

I have responded by acknowledging that people generally do not consciously set out with the intention to cause you hurt, pain or stress. It usually occurs as a result of the person not knowing any better. This awareness when truly embraced will allow you to let go and release the pain and hurt you may have initially experienced.

With this awareness, it truly is all love. Love for my mother and both my fathers. My biological father for the gift of life and clothing, shelter and care as I needed to attend hospital regularly as I suffered from asthma as a child. He did the best that he knew and I am truly grateful.

Love for my spiritual father for introducing me to a way of living that brought me to the place of taking responsibility for my life and how I wanted to show up in the world.

Love for the mother of my children, without whom I could never have been introduced to my best teachers, my children.

Love for my children and the many lessons they taught me as well as the many lessons we learnt together.

Love for all those I have met over the years who have supported me through whatever means they could offer in supporting my vision to empower young people in the UK.

Love for all of the students that I have mentored or coached over the years as I acknowledge fully that the teacher needs the student just as much as the student needs the teacher, for without the student, the teacher with all his knowledge has no purpose. Today as a result, Acie, now a politician in Zimbabwe, is keen for me to come to his town to empower their youth. Who would have thought? And so the story continues...

You must make the decision as I did many years ago that you will not settle. You were born to be successful; in fact, you were born successful. How do I know? It's obvious. Today we know through science that to arrive as a baby you as a tiny sperm had to win literally the race of your life against millions of spermatozoa as you raced to be the first to reach the egg in your mother's womb. So you see, the fact is that you were born a winner.

Find out what success means to you, through the study of you. You are your greatest asset. If you take you for granted, other will also. Find out, explore, discover your gifts, natural talents and abilities and use these to determine what you are passionate about. If you can use this passion to identify a problem in the world and then get the idea that you want to solve this problem, you may well be on your way to growing personal success. Ideas help you form a vision and a vision helps you set your GPS—the voyage can now begin. As you begin to move, you will begin to gain clarity. In truth, regardless what comes your way, positive or negative, once your GPS is set and you're moving, whatever comes your way merely informs you, helping you to gain clarity and more clarity and even more clarity.

Confusion is created through lack of clarity.

The reverse is also true.

Seek clarity in every step of your life's journey and confusion will dissolve.

You must continue to seek this clarity through all adversities, as adversities will surely come. Remember your GPS is set now and you are on your great voyage. As you journey towards your purpose, check your GPS from time to time, but now merely see these adversities when they appear and temporarily throw you off course as a means to help you get clarity—a means to reset your GPS.

Now it's just a game and you are playing to win as you have always done.

With this new knowledge, I'd like you to revisit your list of priorities that you set at the beginning of the book. Now that you have read this book, are you still happy with the current order? I bet you are not. If you are not happy with the order, then go ahead a re-prioritise. This will show you instantly and clearly how much reading this book has impacted the new way in which you see yourself and the world around you.

Save the best for last

Students tell me that once they embark on The GPS mentoring/coaching programme, they suddenly begin to encounter real life situations which test their learning. My response is always the same. I share the story of a driver who one day decides he is gonna change his old car for a new Mercedes, a particular model. The moment that the decision is made, as if by magic the driver seems to see an increased number of that car's make and model all around him. There is no increase in the number of these cars orbiting the driver. But there is an increase in awareness of that car and so by the law as illustrated in this book:

"What you focus on grows."

It is through this very same law that this book came into being. The moment I embraced the idea of writing this book as a tool to support others, in particular young people, then thoughts, ideas and scenarios gravitated toward me, which I in turn wanted to share. It became a perpetual cycle

The journey of writing this book in itself has been a remarkable one that has firmly reinforced for me the idea that it is not possible to out give life. When you give to a cause and purpose bigger than yourself, life has a way of giving back to you through various channels. So it is that I could not complete this book without acknowledging the woman who gently pushed me to getting this book started, Ms Serah Lister. She is a powerful motivational speaker as well as multi-million pound negotiator. Meeting her has been a blessing to my life and the life of Urban Voice UK and hopefully soon Urban Voice Kenya as we look at how to set up a branch there, which is where she originally is from.

During the book writing process, I gave many of the chapters of the book to my intern who at aged 17 was the perfect age to test if the content would resonate. He gave excellent feedback, some positive other not so positive, but still invaluable and as a result I was able to refine the content.

One of his requests was for a questionnaire to accompany each chapter so as to reinforce the learning. If you also think you would benefit from this send us a message after registering at http://www.growpersonalsuccess.com.

After reading the book and working in my office for just 3 months, read an extract from his 3-month report on the impact the experience and the book had on him.

The last three months of mentorship has impacted my life in such a way that I cannot even understand how the basics that I regarded as unimportant could transform the direction my life is heading. One of the things that I couldn't understand before was the importance of speech and utilising words. I have begun to pay more attention to what is being said and as a result, receiving more understanding. This could help me in all aspects of my life, most importantly, the world of work.

How others now see me
There are a lot of people I do not associate myself with anymore because they would hold me back from what I want to achieve and what I have realised in terms of me needing help to build myself up to be successful, in the right way, the legal way, the painstaking and diligent way. The few people that I keep closest to me now think that I am different in terms the way I conduct myself. My closest friend has said, "You think you're a businessman now." My answer was simple. "I've never had the opportunity to show you this side of me."

As I drew nearer to the completion of the book, I received another amazing gift. One of the authors on Raymond Aarons 10x10x10 programme, which is the book writing system I used to write this book, offered to read my book and give me pointers. I gave her my manuscript on Christmas Eve. By 13:00pm on Christmas day, she sent me an email with her comments saying she had read the book.

How? I thought to myself. When I asked her, she explained that my book was so similar to her book, *The Book on Success* by Viv Oliver, that once she started reading she couldn't stop until she had read the whole book, which incidentally took her 5 hours.

On closer examination, we realised that in today's world of business, in order to be successful you must acknowledge that you are a brand and must be aware of your personal brand

The GPS System allows you to first define you and establish your personal brand. *The Book on Success* is like a Part 2, teaching you how to be successful in business.

Viv has become an invaluable support as we now work closely together.

Register at http://www.growpersonalsuccess.com to join my membership club so you can receive up to 30% discounts on business coaching and training delivered by Viv, plus other training from my team of specialists.

If you would like to purchase the 10x10x10 programme to help you write the book that lies inside you, you can register to receive a 30% discount on this book writing system at www.growpersonalsuccess.com.

At the site, you will also be able to register for the range of GPS courses that have been put together if you want to take the next step of Growing Your Personal Success. These are

1. 1-Day introduction course
2. Online course with additional course material
3. 1-Day package for schools, colleges and Universities – consisting of seminar and workshop. Plus
    a. 25 copies Book deal
    b. 50 copies book deal
4. 3-Day weekend course
5. 8-Week course
6. 12-Week course

These courses take you to the next level of The GPS System and are designed to fast track you so that you can benefit from over 50 years of combined research and study.

Through these courses and programmes, you will discover your "5 Pillars". Many people refer to the need to keep Mind, Body and Spirit together, but there are two more pillars which are crucial in understanding how you currently show up in the world and how you want to show up in the world.

The two additional pillars are.

1. Your Social/Emotional State

Life is about relationships and most of us have never consciously learnt how to relate, i.e., often we do not know how to relate with ourselves or our emotions. Is it any wonder then why so many of us struggle in our relationships with others?

2. Your Service/Financial State

You cannot live life without a purpose. Every living person can and must do something so that their life can have meaning. As a result, you should and must consciously give service for which you can and must be remunerated.

The GPS mentoring courses show you how to build on the GPS System, consciously integrating these universal principles with your 5 pillars. When you are able to do this successfully, the results are astounding. Go to the website http://www.growpersonalsuccess.com to watch some of the testimonials.

Over at the site, you will also be able to access all of the books that I have recommended below. Some of these books you might prefer to access as audio books on YouTube or through other sources. One thing is certain—read one of these books each month in this particular order as I have set it so that each book introduces new ideas whilst reinforcing the learning gained throughout the previous book and in 12 months you will be amazed at how differently you think and how differently you see yourself and the world around you.

1. *Rich Dad, Poor Dad* by Robert Kiyosaki
2. *Linchpin: Are You Indispensible?* by Seth Godin
3. *The Richest Man in Babylon* by George Clason
4. *Think and Grow Rich* by Napoleon Hill
5. *7 Habits of Highly Effective People* by Steven Covey
6. *The 8th Habit* by Steven Covey
7. *The Book on Success* by Viv Oliver
8. The *Way Forward* by Bro Ishmael Tetteh
9. *My Deepest Intent* by Deborah Johnson
10. *The Answer Is You: Waking up to Your True Potential* by Michael Beckwith
11. *Start with Why* by Simon Sinek
12. *The New Psycho-Cybernetics* by Maxwell Maltz

As well as joining our membership, if you or a young person you know would like to participate or get involved with Urban Voice UK, here are just some of the various ways in which you can do that

1. Donations—These will be made to the organisation and will be used in delivering a course of activity direct to them. Go to http://www.urbanvoiceuk.com

and press on the donate tab to make a donation or sponsor a young person onto one of our programmes.

2. Staff or volunteer
3. Urban Voice youth council committee
4. Events
5. Supporters/Membership

Read the books I have recommended over 12 months, practice and your mind will be transformed as will the way you view the world.

GPS summit—We are planning to invite some of the authors on the reading list to motivate and inspire you in January 2015. Let us know if this would be of interest to you and reserve a priority seat by registering your email details. Who would you like to see on the Bill?

So there you have it—The GPS System, my gift to you my reader. I'm done and it's now over to you.

What are you gonna do now?

Are you gonna choose to make something happening? Or choose to do nothing.

Even if you choose to do nothing you've made a choice so why not choose to grow and BE somebody.

Nuff Luv
Tony Biola